I0445570

CHANGE YOUR WORDS TO CHANGE YOUR WORLD

A Guide to Breaking Dysfunctional Patterns of Communication in Marriage, Relationships and the Workplace

MELANIE K. HALL
LICENSED CLINICAL PROFESSIONAL COUNSELOR

MJS Book Company LLC

Printed Worldwide
First Printing 2024
First Edition 2024

ISBN: 979-8-9918982-0-1

10 9 8 7 6 5 4 3 2 1

CHANGE YOUR WORDS TO
CHANGE YOUR WORLD

DEDICATION

This book is dedicated to everyone who journeyed with me through every twist and turn along my path. And boy, has it been a journey! Thank you, God, for grace!

To my parents, thank you for everything you've instilled in me, for the lessons you trusted me to learn on my own, and for your spoken and unspoken sacrifice to watch me bloom. I am who I am because of both of you.

To my sisters—Karen, who shared her passion for helping those who need help helping themselves and whose spirit still guides me, and Vickie, who has always been the voice of rebuilding at the weakest points in my life. Your influences are woven into the very fabric of my being.

To my husband, I cannot thank you enough for growing alongside me. My gratitude for your life and love knows no bounds.

To my children, you are my legacy and the reason behind everything I do. You remind me of my purpose and my path. You will always have my unconditional love.

And to my friends, family, colleagues, and educators, thank you for being my community. Your support sharpens me, and your acceptance and guidance sustain me. I am truly grateful for each of you.

TABLE OF CONTENTS

INTRODUCTION

I want you to recall how many times you've had an interaction with someone, had a vision of how it would go, and the outcome be quite the opposite. This was the larger part of my life. I would go into a situation saying to myself, "I will just say ___, and that will open it up." The amount of confusion in the aftermath had me shaking my head, asking, "how in the world did it get to that?" I eventually learned that my emotions were not well-regulated; I communicated my thoughts and feelings from a place of emptiness. Well, let's be honest: I communicated A LOT, but most was emotional vomiting. I was full of emotion but lacked the ability to go from rage to rest in a healthy way. If this sounds familiar to you…. you've opened the right book, and this is where we will start. This is your turning point and, hopefully, your pivotal moment in life.

As a licensed clinical professional counselor, I'm dedicated to helping individuals enhance their communication skills and regulate their emotions. My journey into the world of counseling and mental health began at Roosevelt University in Chicago to a private practice in Homewood, Illinois. I've had the privilege of supporting a diverse population of clients through clinical counseling, personal coaching, and relationship coaching, as well as company trainings and workshops for team building. With years of experience in the field, I've witnessed firsthand the transformative power of effective communication in fostering healthier relationships and emotional well-being. My approach is typically blended with professional expertise and real-world applications that draw on both my formal training and the lessons learned from day-to-day interactions with clients.

What drives me is seeing people transform their relationships by simply talking and listening better. This book is packed with insights, strategies, and practical exercises that I've seen work wonders. My goal is to give you straightforward, no-nonsense advice that you can actually use in your everyday life. Aside from my counseling practice, I am an avid reader, music enthusiast, and a pretty good cook—passions that keep me grounded and continuously learning. Each of these hobbies connects me more deeply with family, the community I serve, and my colleagues, enriching my understanding of the varied human experiences that shape our interactions.

Through this book, I aim to share some of my own personal stories that serve to provide you with how I learned to walk the talk. I deeply value connecting with others, and if you're reading this book, you're likely very similar. My goal is to guide you through refining your communication strategies to build stronger, more fulfilling relationships. Welcome to a conversation about making meaningful changes that can positively impact every aspect of your life.

This book was created to be your roadmap. It's the companion on your journey of exploring your emotional intelligence, communication, and relationship-building. It offers the strategies, insights, and actionable steps to guide your interactions to the favorable outcomes you envision. It will encourage not just conversation but transformation. The chapters in this book will be a resource to enhance your emotional intelligence and navigate communication challenges.

We're going to cover a lot of ground—everything from the common communication traps we all fall into to the ways we can turn those around and build deeper connections. I want to help you have those important conversations that often get overlooked so you can truly understand yourself and others. Welcome to the conversation, the reflection, the action, and a journey of growth. Let's begin.

CHAPTER 1

UNDERSTANDING EMOTIONS AND COMMUNICATION

You've heard the term "emotional intelligence" (EI) tossed around, haven't you? It's become the golden key to unlocking personal and professional success. But what is it, really? For those that do not know, EI is a concept where we are aware of our own feelings, understand them and can express them. But in my opinion, what makes it wonderful is in this intelligence we are also able to recognize what other people might be feeling. So, in a nutshell, EI is about self-awareness, understanding your own emotions, and having the ability to recognize or empathize with others.

This concept closely aligns with the idea of "reading the room." We want to learn to navigate through the human experience with awareness, empathy, and grace. It's not about academic prowess or IQ; it's about understanding, managing, and using emotions in a positive way. EI is at the core of meaningful relationships, effective communication, and personal well-being. In an era where technology seems to reign supreme, the human touch is what truly makes a difference. The rise of EI as a coveted skill isn't coincidental. In workplaces, homes, and social settings, the ability to empathize, connect, and communicate effectively sets individuals apart. It's what machines can't replicate—the delicate layers of human emotions and connections. This is what builds relationships.

So, why all the buzz about EI now? We're all moving so quickly through this digitally connected world, and we are losing the art of basic human connection. It has become increasingly difficult for people to understand and manage emotions. As tasks become more automated, it's our use of uniquely human skills that set us apart— the ability to empathize, to create, and to connect. That's where EI will shine.

Your growth in this area will include increased self-awareness, self-regulation, and better overall social skills. When you increase your awareness of your emotions, you can regulate your emotional responses. Being aware of your own also allows you to empathize with others and may allow you to understand what you observe in others. Increasing your emotional intelligence is a key component of communicating with others effectively and can help build more satisfying social relationships. The beauty of EI is that it's not fixed. You can grow, adapt, and enhance your emotional intelligence with intention and practice.

This reminds me of one of the most chaotic periods in my marriage. We were two working adults with two young kids, a dog, and a home that felt increasingly cramped. Everyone has their own 'stuff,' and the unfortunate thing about it is that it can blind you to your partner. It was that twilight hour when everyone was getting home, and the house buzzed with unfinished homework and dinner preparations. My husband would walk in from work, and while the kids were excited—smiling at the door and in the window—we barely exchanged a glance, offering each other only a dry "hello." He would usually retreat to the basement to unwind, but his time there grew longer each day. When he finally re-emerged, I would bombard him with questions, comments, and my 'stuff,' to which he had little to say. This only fed the tension that was already brewing before he even turned the key in the door.

Can you identify what's happening? When we were in it, we both missed the mark. I could not see that he was drained from his job, which was filled with dissatisfaction, and his two-hour commute had sucked the life out of him long before he pulled into the driveway. He couldn't see that my grind as a realtor, coupled with my life as a student, left me irritable, exhausted, and desperately hoping he'd come home and help pick up the slack. We were having two different experiences in the world, but our stuff interfered with our ability to empathize with the other. Our unacknowledged personal experiences became a barrier to seeing that we each needed the same thing. Unfortunately, our lack of communication and style of communication at the time hurt us more. I was loud, outspoken, and aggressive. He allowed me the space to vent but he knew absolutely nothing about how to defuse the bomb that was ticking. His approach to things was the exact opposite, and often felt dismissive and unempathetic or that he was uninterested. And I wanted a response, some emotion, something that said, "I see you." We were both responding to feelings of being overwhelmed with life and had no capacity to truly listen to the other's pain.

Have you ever encountered someone who just doesn't "get it"? They seem to miss social cues, react impulsively, or seem out of touch with their own feelings. That's often a sign of low emotional intelligence. Understanding the intensity of what you feel and deciphering the reasons behind each emotion is the first step toward mastery. This introspection is like an internal dialogue where you ask yourself, "Why does this frustrate me?" or "Does this feeling have anything to do with the right now or something from my yesteryears?" Just because you experience one or several emotions does not make what's happening true. This is a concept often confusing for people. Although the feelings can be intense, could it be something else fueling the moment?

Building on self-awareness is the art of emotional regulation, a powerful skill that allows you to compose your responses to life's diverse scenarios. Rather than being swayed by the emotions of others, you learn to move with an understanding of your own emotions that will help you adjust your response. Emotional regulation is about balance—managing your impulses, expressing your emotions appropriately, and adapting to the ever-changing tides with grace and poise. In the example I shared, if I had taken a moment to reflect and ask myself a few questions, I could have identified what I needed. What I had not done was give myself permission to take a moment and take care of myself so I could show up and invite a conversation rather than attempting to force an exchange. I unfairly expected him to SEE ME and give me what I needed.

From there, we introduce empathy—the ability to step outside ourselves and enter the emotional worlds of others. It's seeing through another's eyes, feeling with another's heart, and walking a mile in another's shoes. Empathy enriches your interactions and deepens your relationships, creating a connection that is both strong and flexible. If you apply empathy to my situation, you'll see how my "stuff" kept me from recognizing his exhaustion, stress, and overwhelming need for renewal.

The Pillars of Emotional Intelligence (EI)

EI is comprised of four pillars, and each pillar is a step in understanding and harnessing the power of emotions. There is self-awareness, self-regulation, social awareness, and relationship management.

1) **Self-Awareness**: This is the foundation. Recognizing your emotions, understanding why you feel a certain way, and acknowledging how your emotions affect your thoughts and actions. This allows you to be rooted in understanding why you do what you do and say what you say.

2) **Self-Regulation**: Once you're aware, the next step is managing those emotions. This is where you're expressing your feelings appropriately, adapting to changing circumstances, and facing challenges with a level head. Think of this as your base for stress management. It's

difficult to manage stress if you are not able to regulate yourself.

3) **Social Awareness**: This pillar is about adjusting as you observe or experience the emotions of others. It involves empathy, recognizing social dynamics, and understanding the unspoken cues in various settings. This is the epitome of "reading the room" and recognizing a shift in someone's mood or demeanor.

4) **Relationship Management**: The culmination of EI is using your emotional awareness and control to foster healthy, productive relationships in any setting. It's mastering the ability to communicate clearly and resolve conflicts. This is required to live the harmonious life you know you want.

High EI doesn't happen overnight. It's a journey, a continuous process of learning, reflecting, and growing. And just as you get the hang of it in one area, you'll have to reinstate the process again because life happens. Below are a few ways you can embark on this journey.

Mindful Observation: Start by observing your emotional reactions **without judgment**. What triggers them? How do they manifest in your thoughts and actions? What was the moment you went from level five to eight?

Emotion Journaling: Keeping a journal can help you track your emotional triggers and patterns, providing insight into your emotional vault. What have you been holding onto that keeps resurfacing even when it isn't the issue at the present time? Most of us are on a continuous journey of healing from past hurts. Journaling can give you an opportunity to process and purge the recurrent themes.

The Power of Pause: In moments of high emotion, you can practice pausing. This is a brief opportunity to regain clarity and choose a more constructive response. I know, I know; people say that's hard. Yes, it is not easy because it is not a habit you've purposefully formed. At any time you are trying to use a new skill, you must practice it repeatedly. You won't be perfect, but you will reap the benefits when it works well.

Empathy Exercises: Actively work on empathy by putting yourself in others' shoes, especially during times of conflict. You can hold space for someone else and honor your emotions at the same time. This can transform your interactions and relationships. How do you do this? Start by saying, "I'm trying to understand how you feel, but you have to help me do that by using your words."

Challenges and setbacks are opportunities to deepen your EI. Each difficult situation is your chance to practice self-regulation, empathy, and effective communication. Reflect on these moments as lessons in your EI journey.

Finally, the harmonious blend of EI is incomplete without honing your social-emotional skills. These are the tools and techniques that enable you to communicate effectively, resolve conflicts, build strong relationships, and lead with inspiration. Social skills are the outward expression of your internal emotional intelligence, the moment where you display your emotional understanding and control. Integrating EI into your daily life can transform your interactions into meaningful connections. You will get to experience and demonstrate actively listening during conversations, managing stress in high-pressure situations, and being attuned to the emotional climate of your surroundings.

As with any form of intelligence, the enhancement of EI is an ongoing process. It calls for patience, dedication, and a commitment to continuous learning and growth. Through this process, you'll find that your ability to navigate the highs and lows of emotions—both yours and others—becomes one of your greatest strengths, enriching every aspect of your life, from personal relationships to professional endeavors.

Remember, emotional intelligence is not a destination or finish line; it's you deciding to maintain a path of perpetual growth. Each step on this path is a step toward a more aware, controlled, empathetic, and socially adept you.

Takeaways

- EI is your ability to understand and manage your emotions and recognize those of others.

- The demand for EI has skyrocketed as the world becomes more automated and digitally connected.

- Recognizing the signs of low EI (in yourself and others) is the first step toward growth.

- Building EI is a journey of self-awareness, regulation, and empathy.

Enriched Reader Prompts

Self-Reflection: Spend a few minutes each day reflecting on your emotional experiences. What triggered your emotions? How did you respond internally and externally? Think of a situation where you misread someone else's emotions. What was the outcome, and what could you have done differently?

Seek Feedback: Ask trusted friends or colleagues about how you come across in emotional situations. Be open to what they share.

Empathy Practice: Commit to one action this week to enhance your EI. Whether it's pausing to reflect on your feelings, asking for feedback, or practicing empathy, write it down and make it happen.

CHAPTER 2

YOUR COMMUNICATION BLUEPRINT

D on't you wish you had a blueprint? A blueprint to guide you through all the nuances of life. That preparation would be invaluable. We think we know communication because we "talk" every day, but there is no guide that helps us stay in alignment with our core values while we address our unique challenges. This chapter is about creating your own blueprint. One that empowers you to communicate with clarity, confidence, and empathy.

Think of this book as your personalized guide to build your blueprint, tailored to your experiences, values, and goals. Here's how you can start crafting it:

1. Identify Your Core Values:

Begin by understanding what truly matters to you. Your values are the foundation of your blueprint. Whether it's honesty, compassion, respect, or growth, knowing your core values will help you navigate conversations with a strong sense of purpose and integrity. Remember, you have to create this blueprint and create boundaries around it.

2. Set Clear Intentions:

Before engaging in any significant conversation, set clear intentions for yourself. What do you hope to achieve? I often encourage others to use what became helpful for me and that is disclaimers. I might say something like, "I hope you are able to receive this with the love I have for you," or "You are not going to like what I'm about to say, but I hope you can respect it because it is coming from a place of self-care." Are you seeking to resolve a conflict, express your feelings, or share important information? You must know where you plan to go with the conversation. Clear intentions act as a compass, keeping your communication focused and meaningful.

3. Develop Active Listening Skills:

Effective communication is as much about listening as it is about speaking. It is critical because you must listen with the goal of processing what you hear cognitively, not emotionally. Before you can respond or react, I encourage you to pause long enough to repeat what you heard to yourself and the other person. Practice active listening by giving your full attention, acknowledging the speaker's feelings, and responding thoughtfully. This shows respect and fosters a deeper connection.

4. Practice Empathy

Empathy is the ability to understand and share the feelings of another. Put yourself in the other person's shoes and try to see the situation from their perspective. Even if you are the one who has been betrayed, you can still empathize with the discomfort the other person may have about what they did to you. This could sound something like this: "I'm hurt, and I'm angry, and I'm sure you feel crappy about being the one that hurt me." While empathy is often used to build trust, it also opens the door to more compassionate and productive conversations.

5. Enhance Your Emotional Vocabulary

The more accurately you can describe your feelings, the better you can communicate them. When I think of the early years in school, we learned vocabulary words, but I cannot recall using words that would build on my feelings. We also know that most academic settings did not spend a lot of time on social-emotional learning, so we essentially became adults lacking the ability to identify and verbalize our emotions. Expand your emotional vocabulary to include a wide range of emotions far beyond happy, sad, mad, or glad. Learn what each word means and how it may be more precise in describing how you feel. This allows for more precise and effective communication.

6. Seek Feedback and Reflect

Effective communication is a process. Seek feedback from trusted friends, family, or colleagues about your communication style. Your feedback requests are not for affirmation or validation but to be sure you are executing the changes you want to make with your communication. Reflect on your interactions to identify what worked well and what could be improved. Continuous reflection and adjustment will strengthen your blueprint over time.

7. Practice, Practice, Practice

Like any skill, effective communication requires practice. Own it. Engage in conversations with intention, apply what you've learned, and don't be afraid to make mistakes. Each interaction is an opportunity to refine your blueprint and grow as a communicator.

Identify Your Core Values

Understanding what truly matters to you will also drive how effective you are with communication. Your core values are the philosophies that guide your behavior, decisions, and interactions. They're like the roots of a tree. The values will provide stability to every aspect of your life. When you communicate in alignment with your core values, your words carry authenticity and power. Think of the many times you have heard someone speak with conviction in their voice. You sensed that because their belief system reinforced their ability to communicate their position.

Take some quiet time to reflect on your life experiences. Think about the moments when you felt most fulfilled and the situations that caused you the greatest discomfort. What were the common themes? For instance, did you feel proud when you acted with integrity or compassionate when you helped others? These reflections can reveal your underlying values.

Look at the people you admire and respect. What qualities do they personify that resonate with you? Maybe it's their unwavering honesty, their commitment to justice, or their kindness. Often, the traits we admire in others are reflections of the values we hold dear. What's holding you back from demonstrating the same qualities?

Write down all the **values** that come to mind during your reflection. Don't filter yourself; just let the words flow. Once you have a comprehensive list, start narrowing it down. Aim to identify *five to ten* core values that truly resonate with you. These should be the values that you feel deeply connected to and that influence your daily actions. When I think of values, I think of words like accountable, thoughtful, and fair. These values are who you are.

To make your values actionable, define what each one means to you. For example, if 'respect' is a core value, describe what respect looks like in your interactions. Does it mean listening without interrupting, valuing others' opinions, or treating everyone with dignity? By defining your values, you create a clear framework for how you want to communicate and behave.

Sometimes, values can come into conflict. For example, you might value both honesty and harmony, but they may clash in certain situations. There's a time and place for both. Prioritize your values to understand which ones take precedence when conflicts arise. This doesn't mean one value is less important, but knowing your hierarchy can guide you in making tough decisions.

Incorporate your core values into your daily life. Use them as a compass to guide your actions and decisions. For instance, if growth is a core value, seek opportunities for learning and self-improvement. If compassion is important, practice empathy and kindness in your interactions. Living your values consistently builds integrity and trust. This also teaches people how to treat you.

Values can evolve over time; as you grow and your life circumstances change, they shift. Make it a habit to periodically reevaluate your core values and communicate them when necessary to those that are most important to you. Reflect on whether they still resonate with you and if your actions align with them. This ongoing process ensures that your blueprint remains relevant and effective.

By identifying and embracing your core values, you lay a solid foundation for effective communication. Your values act as a guiding light, helping you navigate conversations with authenticity and confidence. They remind you of what's truly important and keep you grounded, even in challenging situations. With a clear understanding of your core values, your words and actions will resonate with integrity, making your communication more impactful and meaningful.

Set Clear Intentions

Clear intentions act as a roadmap for your conversations. They guide you, keep you focused, and ensure your communication aligns with your goals. Before engaging in any significant conversation, ask yourself what you hope to achieve. Are you looking to resolve a conflict, express your feelings, share important information, or make a decision? Knowing your objective helps you stay on track and communicate more effectively. This will help you reduce fillers and saying things that truly don't matter.

Ask for what you want. Be clear with your "no." Vague intentions can lead to misunderstandings. Be specific about what you want to accomplish. For instance, instead of intending to "have a good talk," aim to "understand why my partner feels upset about our recent disagreement." Specificity provides clarity and direction.

Effective communication is a two-way street. I understand that emotions make it difficult to think about the other person but think about the other person's needs, feelings, and perspectives. Setting intentions that consider their viewpoint fosters empathy and collaboration, making the conversation more productive.

Once you've set your intentions, share them with the other person. Be honest and clear. This transparency helps to align expectations and sets the stage for a more open and honest dialogue. For example, you might say, "I'd like to talk about our recent disagreement to understand how we can avoid similar issues in the future." Conversations can take unexpected turns. Stay open to adjusting your intentions as needed. Flexibility allows you to adapt and respond thoughtfully rather than rigidly sticking to a preconceived plan.

Develop Active Listening Skills

While active listening is not a verb, listening is. You must actively do something. It is the cornerstone of effective communication. Stop and ask yourself what you are responding to. If you have difficulty following the person's verbiage, ask them to pause because you've gotten lost along the way, and you're no longer able to follow. Be sure you are not having feelings of inadequacy because you are no longer able to follow. Stating so is communicating. Do not allow them to continue speaking if you are not actively listening. For example, if I am listening to my partner and they seem to have gotten off-topic, I might interrupt and say, "Hold on. Can you pause for a moment because it seems like you just switched gears. Are we still talking about the same thing?" It's not just about hearing words but truly understanding the speaker's message.

In our overstimulated world, giving full attention can be challenging. Put away distractions, make eye contact, and show the person you're speaking to that you're fully present. If you are speaking to someone and they keep intermittently checking their phone or looking at the television, you will likely become upset because you feel dismissed by the lack of their attention. Putting away your phone, muting the television, or turning down the radio demonstrates respect and encourages more meaningful dialogue.

People want to feel heard and understood. Use verbal and nonverbal cues to acknowledge and connect with the speaker's feelings. Nodding, maintaining eye contact, and responding with phrases like "I understand" or "It sounds like you've been struggling" can go a long way in validating their emotions.

Reflecting and paraphrasing shows that you're actively engaged. Summarize what the speaker has said in your own words. For example, "So what I'm hearing is that you felt left out during the meeting?" or "So what I think you said is you expected me to be there at 9, but it frustrated you when I showed up at 10. Is that true?" This not only clarifies understanding but also demonstrates that you're truly listening.

Encourage deeper conversation by asking open-ended questions. These questions can't be answered with a simple "yes" or "no" and invite the person to elaborate. For instance, "Can you tell me more about what happened?" or "How did that make you feel?" It continues to show interest and genuine curiosity about what needs to be resolved at the time.

Interrupting someone can derail the conversation and make the person feel undervalued. Practice patience and let the person finish their thoughts before responding. Think of how you feel when they constantly interrupt you with their thoughts. Controlling your urge to interrupt creates a more respectful and productive dialogue.

Be genuinely curious about the other person's experiences and emotions. Ask questions and listen actively to show that you care. Genuine interest fosters deeper connections, especially if you want the other person to feel valued.

Avoid jumping to conclusions or passing judgment. When you assume to know what the other person is thinking or going to say it immediately creates defensiveness from them. This is very similar to being interrupted. Normalize giving a person the opportunity to finish their thought. I have personally found that allowing this has given space for the person to possibly arrive at an agreement with me. Approach conversations with an open mind, allowing the other person to express themselves freely. Non-judgmental listening creates a safe space for honest dialogue.

Within my marriage, I learned I was not always a safe space for open dialogue. I would jump to conclusions, make assumptions, and finish sentences. My emotions were in full control. Even though I asked for honest responses, I assumed there would be lies long before he completed his sentences. I was met with defensiveness and nonchalant responses. At the time, it added fuel to the fire that was already ablaze. Growth, searching for understanding, and wanting there to be more respect in the marriage moved me to be silent enough to allow him to finish a thought. I had to remember that I was not the only one that felt pain. Empathy and practicing non-judgmental conversations allowed me to listen and provide a safe space.

Practice Empathy

Empathy is a two-way street. Share your own feelings and experiences to create mutual understanding. Allowing someone else to share does not invalidate your own feelings; it just explains why you're having the conversation. Two people can co-exist in the same space and feel two different things. The feelings do not have to align, but both need to be heard. This vulnerability can help bridge gaps and foster a stronger emotional connection.

Enhance Your Emotional Vocabulary

Being able to precisely describe your emotions improves communication. Expand your emotional vocabulary by learning new words that describe various feelings. Instead of just "happy" or "sad," explore terms like "content," "ecstatic," "frustrated," or "melancholic." A richer vocabulary allows for more nuanced expression. Have you ever been in a conversation at work or home and asked yourself (or the other person), "What does that mean?"

That is because there was more expression needed to fill the gaps in communication. Saying you're angry is not enough. Saying you're confused is not enough. Support the chosen words with more explanation. If you are hurt, say what you heard or observed that led to hurt. If you are confused, describe what you understand and what you are still struggling to understand that creates confusion for you. When we can expand our vocabulary, it aids in understanding for both parties. When describing your emotions, use vivid and specific language. Instead of saying, "I'm upset," you might say, "I'm feeling overwhelmed and frustrated because of the project deadline." Specific descriptions provide clarity and help others understand your experience.

Regularly check in with yourself to identify and label your emotions. Journaling can be a helpful tool for this. So often people frown at journaling because it reminds them of the years that little girls kept diaries. What if you changed your perspective about journaling and considered writing notes about your thoughts or experiences? Does that sound different? Journaling is for you to take notes along your journey of life and life change. Reflect on your feelings and write them down, exploring the nuances of each emotion. This practice enhances self-awareness and emotional expression.

Engage in conversations about emotions with trusted friends or family members. Discussing your feelings openly helps to normalize emotional expression and builds your comfort with using a broader range of emotional terms. Continuous improvement in communication requires feedback and reflection. Ask trusted friends, family, or colleagues for honest feedback about your communication style. Encourage them to share specific examples of what you do well and areas where you could improve. This feedback is invaluable for growth.

After significant conversations, take time to reflect. Consider what went well, what didn't, and why. Reflecting on your interactions helps you identify patterns and areas for improvement. Maintain a journal to document your reflections and insights. Write about your experiences, feedback received, and steps you plan to take to improve. A journal provides a tangible record of your progress and keeps you accountable.

Seek Feedback and Reflect

Based on feedback and reflection, set specific goals for improving your communication skills. For instance, you might aim to practice active listening more consistently or to express your emotions more clearly. Clear goals provide direction and motivation for growth.

Acknowledge and celebrate your progress, no matter how small. Recognizing your improvements boosts confidence and encourages continued effort. Celebrate milestones and the positive impact your enhanced communication skills have on your relationships.

Practice, Practice, Practice

Like any skill, effective communication requires consistent practice. Here's how to incorporate practice into your daily life: Look for moments to engage in meaningful conversations. Whether it's discussing a topic with a friend, resolving a conflict, or expressing your feelings, each interaction is a chance to practice and refine your skills.

Practice challenging conversations through role-playing. Enlist a friend or family member to act out different scenarios with you. This safe and controlled environment allows you to experiment with different approaches and receive immediate feedback.

Observe skilled communicators in action. Is there someone you respect in your circle who demonstrates the level of communication you wish to use? Pay attention to how they listen, respond, and navigate conversations. Learn from their techniques and incorporate what resonates with you into your own communication style. If you're able, ask them how they developed the patience to listen and reflect during conversations.

Consider enrolling in communication courses or workshops, especially in the workplace. These structured learning environments provide valuable insights, techniques, and opportunities for practice. Courses can also offer feedback from instructors and peers.

Regularly reflect on your communication experiences and adjust your approach as needed. Flexibility and willingness to adapt are key to continuous improvement. Each conversation is an opportunity to learn and grow.

By following these detailed steps, you can create a robust blueprint for effective communication. Each element builds on the others, helping you communicate with clarity, confidence, and empathy. Remember, effective communication is a journey, not a destination. With your personalized blueprint, you'll be well-equipped to navigate the complexities of life and build stronger, more meaningful relationships.

Our communication style says a lot about us. Are you direct and to the point, or do you prefer to soften your words with stories and analogies? Do you tackle issues head-on, or do you approach them more guardedly? Recognizing your style is the first step in honing your communication skills.

Even the most eloquent speakers have room for improvement. Reflect on past interactions, moments when you felt misunderstood, when conversations didn't go as planned, or when your words didn't align with your intentions. These reflections can reveal valuable insights into areas ripe for growth. Active listening is the cornerstone of meaningful interaction. Strive not just to hear but to understand the essence of what's being communicated. Sometimes, we may lack the understanding, but with empathy and respect we can approach each conversation with a level of respecting differing viewpoints and emotional states. If you are unclear about what the person is saying in front of you, ask for clarity, not just for yourself, but to let them know you need more information. Once you are clear about their message you can now be clear and concise with yours. Avoid ambiguity and ensure your words align with your intended message.

The blueprint or steps you create for yourself should be tailored to your needs, goals, and the unique contexts in which you find yourself. Consider adjusting your communication style to suit different settings such as the workplace, home, or social situations. Within the interactions what do you aim to achieve? Do you want to persuade, comfort, or connect? And incorporate mechanisms for feedback, allowing you to gauge the effectiveness of your communication and adjust as needed.

You've read a lot here, and there's a lot to explore. Start small, focusing on one or two key areas. Practice, reflect, and refine. Remember, effective communication is a dynamic skill, evolving as we grow and as our relationships deepen.

Takeaways

- Crafting a personal communication blueprint empowers you to navigate interactions with intention and effectiveness.

- Understanding your communication style and identifying areas for growth are foundational steps.

- Principles like active listening, empathy, and clarity are integral to your blueprint.

- Implementing your blueprint involves practice, feedback, and continuous refinement.

Enriched Reader Prompts

1. Communication Style Reflection: Identify your dominant communication style and an instance where it was particularly effective or ineffective. What can you learn from this reflection?

2. Blueprint Goal Setting: Choose one communication goal for the upcoming week. It could be improving active listening, expressing empathy, or being more concise. Plan specific actions to work toward this goal.

3. Feedback Request: After a significant conversation, ask a trusted friend or colleague for feedback on your communication. What insights do they offer? How can this feedback inform your blueprint?

CHAPTER 3

RECOGNIZING AND RESHAPING LEARNED BEHAVIOR

At the core of emotional intelligence lies the power of self-regulation. Self-regulation puts you in the driver's seat of your emotional journey, steering your responses rather than being at the mercy of your impulses. Self-regulation doesn't mean suppressing your feelings; it cultivates recognizing, understanding, and channeling them in constructive ways.

Have you ever been in the room with someone arguing, and you are pensive because you can feel the tension in the room and anticipate an escalation? You know it is only a matter of time before someone says something so hurtful that the other person will "become undone." It's as if your emotions are like waves in the ocean and in that moment, you see the waves turn into a tsunami. The emotions fill the room, and there is now no concern for who else is in the room, who hears, who sees—only behavior. You see the tears, and you hear the voices rise, the screams, the flailing hands, the stomping feet, and the bulging eyes. Without self-regulation, you are likely experiencing feelings of unrest and the urge to do something to restore calm. With self-regulation, you can feel a sense of centering even when others are not and mindfully put boundaries in place for your own emotional safety. This skill is crucial because it impacts every aspect of your life—from personal relationships to professional success, from your inner peace to your public interactions.

Think of the situation described above. It's that moment when emotions don't just rain; they pour. When feelings don't just speak, they scream. Emotional dysregulation can be turbulent and overwhelming, often leaving us and those around us exhausted and confused in the aftermath of its storm. It's characterized by an inability to influence or control one's emotional responses, leading to reactions that are out of proportion with the agitator.

Emotional dysregulation is usually exhibited as sudden, intense emotional responses that might seem excessive. It can stem from a variety of sources, including stress, unresolved trauma, or even innate temperament. Recognizing these patterns is essential—they're signposts indicating where our emotional intelligence journey needs to focus. As a clinician who focuses on the whole person, this is where there might be an inquiry about hormone imbalances, unchecked physical health issues, behavioral side effects of medication, unresolved or complicated grief, patterns of codependency, and other chronic issues that can derail the natural growth path of emotional health. As children, we are not taught how to verbalize feelings. We often learn sad, glad, happy, and mad. We pick up some words along the way, but the one that everyone understands is anger. When anger becomes the one emotion you know how to express (and it's uniquely universal), the other emotions seem to become of lesser value.

Self-regulation is the process that allows us to navigate the waters of our emotions effectively. While it sounds simple, it's the ability that lets us recognize the rise of emotions within us and choose how to roll with them, not against them. It includes the following:

1. **Mindfulness**: Adopting a non-judgmental awareness of the present moment that helps us identify and accept our emotional state. This means allowing yourself to have an inner dialogue about the people around you, the place you are in, and the things that impact you.

2. **Strategic Response**: Choosing a course of action aligned with your values and the demands of the situation rather than being led by the uproar of our feelings. If you suspect you've been wronged, and you believe you have all the information to make an informed decision, think about the outcome you desire and align your response and reactions to that outcome. Anything else would be out of alignment with your value system.

3. **Soothing Techniques**: Implementing strategies that calm the physiological arousal, such as deep breathing, progressive muscle relaxation, or grounding exercises. Do you know what calms you? This is not a rhetorical question. Some of

us are so accustomed to being on high alert that rest seems like the calm before the storm rather than just calm. When you find yourself in a space where you need to find an internal source of peace and calm, you must know how to source it. For example, if I am headed into a meeting where I suspect there will be untruths and manipulation, I will be sure to flood myself with messages that allow me to speak my truth, enforce boundaries, and move at my pace to regulate my emotions.

Transitioning from dysregulation to self-regulation is not short for suppression; it's how you achieve your transformation. As you practice the tips outlined in this book, you are learning to moderate your emotional responses in ways that serve you and your relationships better.

1. **Recognize and Acknowledge**: Begin by acknowledging your emotions without shame or judgment. Recognizing your feelings is the first step toward managing them effectively.

2. **Understand the Triggers**: Dig deep into the causes of your emotional responses. You will have to pause yourself early enough in the emotional escalation to do this. Waiting is counterproductive. Your early detection signs give you wiggle room. You know your landmines better than anyone else. What are the common threads that lead to dysregulation?

3. **Develop Coping Strategies**: Equip yourself with a toolkit of coping strategies. These might include taking time out,

engaging in physical activity, or seeking supportive conversation.

Embracing self-regulation is a transformative journey from reactivity to proactivity. It's about moving from being at the mercy of our emotional storms to navigating them with skill and grace.

1. **Proactive Planning**: Anticipate situations that might lead to dysregulation and plan your strategy in advance. Have a plan on how you will maintain your optimism and avoid being manipulated or mishandled by others.

2. **Emotional Agility**: Cultivate the ability to move fluidly between different emotional states, understanding that emotions are transient and manageable. Remember that it's okay that something or someone "rubbed you the wrong way;" just know you don't have to stick with that emotion the rest of the day. You have the power to change it; reset!

3. **Seek Support**: Remember that the journey is not a solitary one. Support from loved ones or professionals can be invaluable. Sometimes, it's good to have an ally with you when you are going into environments with people that are not your favorites. Your support system can remind you to reset and focus on the positives around you.

The first step in mastering self-regulation is identifying your emotional triggers. Unfortunately, the word trigger has become overused yet it's one of the best descriptions for what I would call emotional landmines or sore spots. These triggers are not visible on the surface, but they are sensitive to the slightest pressure. When they are inadvertently activated, they can cause explosive emotional reactions that are out of proportion to the triggering event. Understanding these sore spots is crucial because it helps us negotiate our interactions more cautiously and thoughtfully.

By recognizing our triggers as these hidden hazards, we can work on defusing them with awareness and care, reducing the chances of emotional upheaval in our day-to-day interactions. Triggers can be anything from specific words, situations, or actions that evoke a strong emotional response. Most people you interact with are not aware that you have these unhealed battle wounds. So, when someone does something that is disrespectful or mistreats you, they may not realize you have a long-standing history of feeling mistreated and disrespected. These are deeply personal and often rooted in past experiences, beliefs, or unmet needs.

1. **Reflection**: Spend time reflecting on moments when you've felt a strong emotional surge. What prompted it? Identifying patterns can provide valuable insights.

2. **Journaling**: Keeping a journal of your emotional triggers and reactions can be a transformative tool. It allows you to track patterns and gain clarity on your emotional landscape.

Strategies for Effective Self-Regulation

1. **Breathing Techniques**: In moments of emotional intensity, breathing slowly and deeply can help center your thoughts and calm your nervous system. This will require complete self-control, but the more you do it, the more it becomes a habit.

2. **Mindfulness and Meditation**: Regular practice of mindfulness and meditation can enhance your ability to observe your emotions without immediately reacting to them. This does not mean that while you are in a dispute, you stop and start the meditation. This might require you to take a break away from the person(s) to focus on calming techniques or a reduction in stimuli. For example, you step out of a warm room and find a cooler room, get a hot or cold beverage, or even remove a layer of clothing. The point is you may have to make some adjustments for yourself to reduce the effects of the triggers.

3. **Cognitive Reappraisal**: This involves reframing your thoughts about a situation to manage your emotional response. It's about seeing the glass half full rather than half empty. How many times have you reflected and thought about a disagreement only to see the situation much differently than before? This usually happens in the aftermath. The goal is to learn to reframe the details of a situation in real time to help you de-escalate and regulate.

4. **Problem-Solving**: You can also call this conflict resolution skills. Instead of stewing in your emotions, focus on actionable steps you can take to address the underlying issue or improve the situation, even if it is a temporary fix. What is the real problem? What can you actively control in the situation?

Incorporating the ability to regulate your emotions into your life can be transformative. Start small, with one or two techniques, and gradually build your "toolbox." Consistency is key. It took me quite some time to learn what triggers me to escalate, regulate myself, and improve my EI. Be kind and patient with yourself.

Real-life application of self-regulation can be seen in how you handle criticism, manage stress, or navigate conflicts. It takes time to learn how to choose your battles, knowing when to speak up and when to let go, and keeping your focus on the bigger picture.

Takeaways

- Emotional dysregulation is a common challenge that can disrupt personal peace and relationships.

- Self-regulation serves as a counterbalance to emotional dysregulation, providing the tools to manage intense emotions.

- Bridging the gap between dysregulation and self-regulation involves mindfulness, understanding triggers, and developing coping strategies.

- The transformative journey from reactivity to proactivity in emotional responses is a key aspect of emotional intelligence.

Enriched Reader Prompts

1. Emotional Awareness Log: For the next week, keep a log of instances of emotional dysregulation. Note the trigger, the emotions felt, and your response.

2. Coping Strategy Development: Identify one coping strategy you can use when you feel dysregulated. Plan how you will implement this strategy in a real-world scenario.

3. Reflect on Support Systems: Consider the support systems you have in place for moments of dysregulation. How might you strengthen these supports or seek new ones?

CHAPTER 4

CONVERSATIONAL PITFALLS

In the countless types of human interaction, communication is the thing that either brings us together or separates us from finding connection and understanding. It's not just the words we use but how we say them, why we say them, and the spaces we create for others to speak. Meaningful communication transcends the mere exchange of information; it encourages empathy, builds trust, and nurtures relationships.

Your communication skills and style are at the core of all the exchanges you have. Of course, you are aware there is verbal and nonverbal communication, but I want you to think about your style of communication. This is yet another concept where you need to be keenly aware of how others see you, which is different than caring what people think about you. You have to ask if people receive you and perceive you the way you intended.

I grew up on the south side of Chicago. Growing up in the inner-city and navigating public transportation forced you to develop a tough exterior that could or would keep you from being a victim of a crime. The goal was to maintain that tough exterior if you had to walk the streets, ride the train or the bus, or even stand around and talk to friends. Our facial expressions were tight and verbal communication was very limited to keep distance from someone you did not know. An example like this is important because when people have had to communicate strength or a hardness on an ongoing basis, they might carry that style of communication into places where it is not necessary. That persona has become normalized and a habit. For those who still carry that persona, you must become self-aware enough to know that it's there. The unfortunate truth is it's not a universal experience; it's relative. Some of the people you meet in life will sense the tension, defensiveness, and lack of trust but have no way to discern whether it is personal or not.

Some of the most common barriers to communication are cultural differences, language barriers, and even physical barriers. However, emotional barriers often appear not just in intimate relationships but also in friendships, family interactions, and workplace environments. If you are not able to communicate your boundaries, wants, and needs without allowing your strong emotions to interfere, you will have difficulties in your relationships.

Picture this exchange. Your coworker is having a relatively benign conversation with another coworker. Without any warning, one of them begins to raise their voice and use words that would draw concern of a heated debate. During the aftermath, the person on the receiving end of the aggression says, "I don't know what happened; we were fine, and I told her I needed it by the end of the day, and she snapped at me." The only conclusion to draw from what was heard and the observation is that the other person was already frustrated and angry at a completely different source. The coworker had no clue there was something else in the exchange with them until there was an escalation.

We do not know what people are dealing with internally before striking up a conversation with them. We must understand that sometimes people are barely holding it together, even at work. However, the coworker had a responsibility to say, "Can we please discuss this later today or tomorrow? I have a lot happening outside of work, and it's distracting my ability to meet deadlines." There might have been pushback, but the conversation could have changed, and it may have become more empathetic and supportive versus one-sided about the needs of the business.

There are four communication styles that we will explore here. Passive, passive-aggressive, aggressive, and assertive communication is in all of us, and we demonstrate all four in a multitude of ways every day, whether it is intentional or unintentional. Do you know which one you primarily use? The goal is for you to identify which one you predominately use and make sure it's appropriate for you and your desired goal.

- Passive communication is a style of communicating in which individuals demonstrate patterns of avoidance and expressing their feelings.

- Passive aggressive communication is a style of communicating in which individuals practice denying their feelings of anger or discontentment with others verbally or behaviorally.

- Aggressive communication is a style of communicating in which individuals do not take into account the welfare, feelings, and/or the opinions of others. They are often combative and forceful, leaving no safe space for others to respond.

- Assertive communication is a style of communicating in which individuals advocate for themselves in a calm and positive way without trespassing on the rights and feelings of others. This style of communication is often confused with aggressive because it is direct and lacks verbal fillers. However, when used effectively, words spoken are clear, concise, and void of confusion or wavering.

Passive communication will demonstrate a pattern of avoidance. When you are actively passive in your communication, you will avoid dealing with the feelings of others as well as expressing your own. Unfortunately, interpersonal communication skills are rarely taught in school. We learn them independently. It's characterized by a pattern of avoidance, indirectness, and a submissive demeanor. Sociologically speaking, passive communicators might prioritize group harmony over individual expression, but this can lead to imbalanced relationships where their needs are consistently overlooked. Passive communicators often stand on the edge of conversations. They tend to agree outwardly while disagreeing on the inside. It's like saying "yes" when every fiber of your being is screaming "no." This style of communication is marked by a reluctance to express thoughts, feelings, or needs directly. It's as if the words get lost in translation, not quite making it from the heart to the tongue.

You might ask why some folks tend to lean toward passivity. It's like a defense mechanism or a shield. Maybe it's fear of conflict, rejection, or a deeply rooted belief that their thoughts and feelings don't hold weight. They might have learned early on that silence was safer, or they've been steamrolled in conversations before, learning to just go with the flow to avoid making waves.

The trouble with passive communication is that it's like a slow leak in a tire—it doesn't fix itself, and over time, it can leave you stranded. It often leads to a build-up of unspoken words and unexpressed emotions. And what happens when emotions pile up like unread letters? They can turn into resentment, anxiety, or even a profound sense of isolation.

So, what's the takeaway? If you find yourself in the passive communication camp, know this: your voice is your power. It's the instrument of your thoughts and the ambassador of your feelings. Cultivating a more assertive style is not about being loud or dominant; it's about valuing your own perspective as much as you value the perspectives of others. Find that sweet spot where your needs and the needs of others coexist in harmony. Remember, every voice, including yours, adds value.

Passive-aggressive communication is like a shadow dance. This is the art of saying one thing and meaning another, of concealing disapproval or resentment in the appearance of apparent acquiescence. Imagine agreeing to a request with a smile, all the while knowing you have no intention of following through or offering a compliment laced with a cutting undertone that leaves the receiver unsettled.

This communication style is often the language of the unheard— the ones who feel they can't express their anger or frustration openly. So, they express it covertly. It's the resistance and silent rebellion that creates the greatest issue. The frustrating "yes" that really means "no," the gift that comes with strings attached, the "I'm fine" when disgruntlement is brewing just beneath the surface.

Sociologically, passive-aggressive behavior can be seen as a coping mechanism, one that arises in environments where open expression of disagreement is discouraged or penalized. It's a byproduct of power imbalances, unmet expectations, and conflicts that simmer but never come to a boil. It can be the hallmark of a culture that values politeness over directness, where the social cost of conflict is deemed too high.

But here's the issue: passive-aggressive communication doesn't just fail to resolve the underlying issue—it often exacerbates it. Like planting seeds of mistrust and confusion, watering them with every sarcastic remark, every non-committal agreement, and every task left undone. If you catch yourself in the passive-aggressive patterns of behavior, it's time for a change. I encourage you to begin by giving yourself permission to feel your feelings, recognize your needs, and assert them openly. You can begin breaking the cycle of indirect expression and cultivating the courage to address issues head-on with clarity and honesty.

Transforming passive-aggressive tendencies into assertive communication will feel like turning on a light switch to bring light into a room. It's not easy. It requires you to tap into strength and self-reflection. But the result? Clearer relationships, less internal turmoil, and a sense of integrity in the way you interact with the world. Remember, every word you speak is a layer of transparency in your relationships. Build with intention, with respect, with truth—build with assertive communication, and watch your relationships transform.

Aggressive communication is like a very bad storm. It's forceful, unyielding, and often leaves a trail of disruption behind. Imagine a conversation where one voice doesn't just create more tension; it tries to eliminate the tension by adding more force. This would be the voice of someone who's not just sharing their perspective but pushing it, insisting on it, and demanding that it takes center stage.

When someone communicates aggressively, they're standing their ground—in fact, they're taking ground, sometimes without regard for the other person standing on it. It's usually void of a solution and more about a demonstration of power, a verbal arm-wrestling match where winning isn't just the goal; it's the only outcome they'll accept. Aggressive communication is often linked to a level of hierarchical dynamics and power plays. It reflects a worldview where dialogue is a zero-sum game, and every interaction is an opportunity to assert dominance. You can see it in the boardroom where one person talks over another, in a household where one voice silences the rest, or in any space where a conversation turns into a one-way street. The escalation is used as a tool to either make something happen or stop something from happening.

Aggressive behavior is very uncomfortable to watch, especially when it leads to violence. To understand the impact of aggressive behavior, consider this real-life example: A group of friends was out enjoying drinks, cracking jokes, and being young and uninhibited when one couple, clearly having a disagreement off to the side, quickly escalated into a violent confrontation. He hit her—hard. She tried to run, but he grabbed her, dragged her to the ground, and punched her as she cowered beneath a nearby car. The men struggled to stop him; he was uncontrollable for a while, but eventually, they managed to intervene. The aftermath left everyone baffled.

When working with people who have a history of abuse or have difficulty managing their anger, I always ask, "Have you scared yourself yet?" because that is often when individuals will seek help. When they realize they could have gone further had they not been stopped.

Let's talk about the repercussions of mismanaged and unmanaged anger. The issues ripple out like a tsunami. Relationships can be strained or broken under the weight of words delivered harshly. Opportunities for genuine connection and understanding can be lost along the way. And the aggressive communicator is often left wondering why they're met with resistance or why their relationships lack depth. The lack of control leads to job losses, poor health, fractured relationships, and poor coping skills. The number of organic, joyful interactions that could be experienced is overshadowed. The unfortunate part is that people start to remember more of what they do not like about you versus what they do like or love about you.

Moving from aggression to assertive communication is not easy, but it goes from talking at a person to talking with a person. The shift involves recognizing that true strength in communication doesn't lie in volume, control, or force but in the ability to articulate your needs and opinions while also valuing those of others. Getting to a point where you are learning to exchange ideas without turning those ideas into weapons.

If while reading this book you realize that your communication style leans toward aggressive, consider it an invitation to explore the strength of vulnerability, the power of empathy, and the impact of a voice that doesn't just speak but also listens. It's an invitation to transform your life and those around you to purposeful growth and calm.

Assertive communication stands out. It's the sweet spot between passive silence and aggressive dominance. Picture speaking your truth but with the kind of impact that doesn't overshadow someone else's voice. When you're assertive, you are the driver of your own conversation. You're not asking nor giving permission to express thoughts or feelings; you own yours and your counterpart owns theirs. You embrace the ability to participate in an exchange with a kind of respect that elevates the dialogue. You understand that it isn't about being the loudest in the room; it's about being clear, direct, and honest, all while giving space for others to do the same.

So, why is assertiveness your goal? Because it's the language of self-respect and respect for others. If your goal is to build relationships, this is how you set boundaries without building walls. In the verbal portion of engagement, assertive communication is like moving in a level of affirmation together with the other person.

In the realm of communication, assertiveness is seen as the golden thread of self-expression. It creates balance in the voice of leaders, advocates, or anyone who's ever stood up for what they believe in without stepping on others. The assertive communicator knows that every person's perspective is valuable in the greater human experience. They communicate with intention and respect, which creates a stronger connection.

The first time I realized I was not verbalizing my "no" effectively was with a gentleman who came into my office unsolicited to sell products. I told him, "No, thank you," but of course, as a salesman, he attempted to turn my no into a yes. Because I was distracted and had something to do, I was able to shoo him off and get back to work. He showed up the next day with the same offer with the same energy. He was nice and I allowed him to go through his process, but I was getting increasingly annoyed. I said no thank you twice, but he kept talking. I realized I was angry—not with him, but with myself. I said "no," but I wasn't assertive. It was passive, and I left room for interpretation with the no I gave him. I cared more about his passion for selling than my motivation to get back to what I was doing. I then realized I had to just say it. I said, "I don't mean to be rude, but I have to interrupt you. I appreciate your effort, but it really is no for me. I don't need it, and I don't want it, and I have to get back to work." He thanked me for my honesty and wished me well. I had to remember that assertiveness would also require me to enforce my boundaries even if it would disappoint the other person.

Here's the truth—assertiveness can be learned. It can be taught and exercised like a muscle; the more you use it, the stronger it gets. Start small; voice an opinion, express a need, and say "no" when you need to. Every time you activate assertiveness, you're not just communicating; you're declaring that you and your conversation partners are worth being heard. Remember, assertiveness isn't just a communication style; it's a way of moving through the world. It allows you to show up for yourself and for others. It's how you become not just heard but understood and respected.

Before we can master the art of meaningful communication, we must recognize the barriers that stand in our way:

1. Listening to Respond vs. Listening to Understand: Unfortunately, we often listen with the intent to reply, not to comprehend. This can lead to misunderstandings and a lack of genuine connection.

2. Assumptions and Judgments: Preconceived notions about others can cloud our communication, leading to biased interactions.

3. Non-Verbal Cues and Cultural Differences: Most communication is nonverbal. Ignoring body language, tone

of voice, or cultural nuances can lead to misinterpretations and conflict.

Principles of Meaningful Communication

1. Active Listening: Engage fully, offer your undivided attention, and reflect on what you've heard to ensure clarity and understanding.

2. Empathy: Strive to understand the feelings and perspectives of the other person, even if you don't agree. As you hear words that describe emotion, recognize their feelings.

3. Clarity and Conciseness: Be clear and to the point. Ambiguity can lead to confusion and misinterpretation.

4. Openness and Honesty: Share your thoughts and feelings openly but with consideration for the other person's feelings.

Creating an environment where open, honest communication can flourish is essential. Imagine how many conflicts could be avoided by activating these elements. This involves:

- Psychological Safety: Ensure that all parties feel safe to express themselves without fear of judgment or reprisal.

- Respect and Valuing Diversity: Embrace and respect different viewpoints and communication styles.

- Patience and Flexibility: Recognize that meaningful communication takes time and may require adjusting your approach based on the situation and the individual.

Meaningful communication is not a one-size-fits-all skill; it needs to be adapted to different contexts:

- In Personal Relationships: It's about deepening connections and understanding, expressing needs and desires, and resolving conflicts constructively.

- In the Workplace: It involves clear directives, active listening to team members, and fostering an inclusive environment that values each person's input.

- In Public and Social Settings: It's about being mindful of cultural norms, respecting diverse perspectives, and engaging in dialogues that promote mutual understanding.

Takeaways

- Meaningful communication is the cornerstone of effective and fulfilling human interaction.

- Recognizing and overcoming barriers to communication is crucial for fostering meaningful exchanges.

- Embracing principles such as active listening, empathy, and clarity enhances the quality of our conversations.

- Adapting communication styles to suit different contexts and relationships is key to successful interactions.

Enriched Reader Prompts

1. Reflect on a recent conversation that felt particularly meaningful. What elements made it so? Was it the depth of

the topic, the way both parties listened, or the feeling of being understood?

2. Identify a recent communication breakdown. Consider the barriers that might have contributed to this breakdown. How could principles of meaningful communication have altered the outcome?

3. Commit to one change in your communication style this week. It could be making an effort to listen more actively, to express your thoughts more clearly, or to approach conversations with more empathy. Note the impact of this change on your interactions.

CHAPTER 5

ACTIVE LISTENING

It is amazing that within the fibers of human interaction, listening is not the mainstay. It's seen as a passive act, but listening is a verb; it is something that requires action. It should always be engaged. It's a silent strength that can build rather than destroy. Listening with intention is fully immersing yourself in the other person's words, emotions, and unspoken messages. The unspoken messages require you to ask questions for clarity, not assumptions that fill in the gap of your confusion. Listening is also an act of empathy, an offering of your presence, and a validation of their experiences, even if the experience is different than yours.

Listening, truly listening, is an art that many of us think we're good at—until we're put to the test. Similarly to cooking, everyone believes they're a great cook until they have to do the things that cooks do. In most relationships where emotions tend to arise, listening becomes increasingly difficult. It can demand more of us than we often realize.

We're living in a world that is quite loud, and everyone wants to be booked and busy. These days, we are bombarded by the sounds of pings, rings, and notifications, each vying for our attention. Most of our brain waves are fragmented by an excessive amount of stimuli. Inside this digital bubble, the soft, subtle sound of a human voice asking to be heard can get lost and overshadowed. It's no surprise that a lot of people report feeling overwhelmed by information, and others complain of not feeling heard. The art of listening doesn't just compete with the noise around us; it battles the noise within us.

Ever tried to listen to someone while you have a proverbial ticker tape running in your head or racing thoughts? Did you find it difficult? Our minds are naturally active, often wandering through the past, rushing to the future, or thinking of responses before the other person has even finished their sentence. We are literally responding to snippets and fragments, especially in our intimate relationships. We believe we can finish their sentences and predict responses. Have you ever tried to listen to someone on the phone in a crowded, loud room? Impossible, right? Most of us are on autopilot, and autopilot mode does not make us a great listener.

Our emotions and egos can act like filters on what we see, hear, feel, and think. These filters distort everything! If someone's words poke our pride or stir up emotions, our ability to listen can short-circuit. We're wired to respond to threats, and sometimes, we mistakenly perceive certain words or nonverbal behavior as just that. It's a defense mechanism, one that doesn't always serve us well.

Multitasking might seem practical and, at times, obligatory, especially in the business world. Multitasking silences everything around you, making you deaf because your brain is already overwhelmed with keeping track of several things. Our brains aren't wired to fully focus on multiple streams of information simultaneously. When we attempt to split our attention, we're not listening; we're just hearing noise. This reminds me of when I speak with couples, where one of the issues in the relationship is when conversations are initiated. Engaging in a conversation with someone who is preparing for a trip, watching their favorite TV show, or attending a crowded event is unlikely to go well. It will go better if you ask, "When is a good time for us to talk?" Conversely, if you want to actively listen to the other person, you must say, "This is not the best time because I can't focus on this conversation the way you need me to."

So, how do we turn this ship around? We start by acknowledging that listening is a skill—a muscle that needs regular workouts. We make it count by making it a practice, carving out spaces for quiet, tuning into the present, and reminding ourselves that in every conversation, there's an opportunity to connect, learn, and grow. You do not have to ignore your thoughts and feelings, but you do need to take your time after the other person has spoken to process what you heard. Listening closes the gap to understanding in all types of relationships, from the personal to the professional. By honing our listening skills, we're not just hearing more; we're deepening our connections with the world and its inhabitants.

True listening extends beyond the ears to the heart and mind. It involves:

1. Full Presence: When you are giving your undivided attention, free from distractions, you are signaling to the speaker that they are valued. Imagine how it feels when someone comes into the room, puts their phone in their pocket, and takes a seat to ask you, "How are you?" You immediately feel intentionality in their presence.

2. Nonverbal Engagement: Making eye contact, nodding, and other nonverbal cues show you are engaged and empathetic. Adults and children alike understand that eye contact is an act of full engagement.

3. Withholding Judgment: Approaching each conversation with an open mind, free from preconceived notions or biases.

Barriers to Effective Listening

Several obstacles can hinder our ability to listen with intention:

1. Internal Distractions: Personal biases, preoccupations, or the rehearsal of your response while the other person is speaking. Ask yourself if you are coming to conversations with a judgment of the person, coming with a negative disposition that has nothing to do with the person you're speaking with, or if the timing is right.

2. External Distractions: Environmental noise, technology, or other external factors that divert your attention. Sometimes,

we have to admit there is too much going on in our environments that do not promote intentional conversation. Sports in the background, other people talking, or even an incessantly barking dog might impact your ability to concentrate on the topic.

3. Emotional Reactivity: Strong emotional reactions to certain topics that can cloud your ability to listen objectively. You must regulate your feelings because the filter, as mentioned before, becomes obscured.

Cultivating the Skill of Intentional Listening

Like any skill, intentional listening can be developed and refined through practice:

1. Mindfulness Practice: Enhancing your ability to be present in the moment can significantly improve your listening skills.

2. Active Engagement: Encourage the speaker by asking open-ended questions and paraphrasing their points to ensure understanding.

3. Emotional Regulation: Learning to manage your emotional reactions, especially during challenging conversations, to maintain focus on the speaker's message.

True listening involves tuning into not just what is said but how it's said—the tone, the pauses, and the unspoken emotions. It's about reading between the lines and being attuned to the message behind the words.

When you listen with intention:

- You foster deeper connections where people feel seen and heard, which deepens relationships.

- You enhance understanding and gain a clearer understanding of the other person's perspective, emotions, and needs.

- You also resolve conflicts more effectively because solutions can be more easily identified. The core issues and emotions are discussed and not passed over.

Takeaways

- Intentional listening is a cornerstone of meaningful communication and empathy.

- Overcoming barriers to listening can enhance both personal and professional relationships.

- The practice of intentional listening involves full presence, active engagement, and emotional regulation.

- The impact of truly listening extends far beyond the conversation, fostering deeper connections and understanding.

Enriched Reader Prompts

1. Practice Mindful Listening: Choose a conversation each day to practice full, mindful listening. Note any challenges you

face and the impact of your focused attention on the interaction.

2. Reflect on Nonverbal Cues: After a significant conversation, reflect on the nonverbal cues you observed. What additional insights did they provide into the speaker's emotions or message?

3. Identify a Barrier: Think of a personal barrier to effective listening you've encountered. Outline a plan to address this barrier in future conversations.

CHAPTER 6

EMOTIONAL REGULATION

Emotional resilience and adversity go hand in hand. Navigating the storms that emerge from simply living life requires strength and flexibility. What we learn keeps us feeling grounded and leveled through life's ups and downs.

Because life is constantly changing and challenges and setbacks are par for the course, resilience is your anchor. It's what enables you to face difficulties with courage, adapt to new circumstances, and find growth and meaning in adversity. We do not build resilience to avoid the storms; we build it because as life continues, the storms will come, and we have to pivot.

Resilience is the ability to bounce back from adversity, adapt to change, and keep going in the face of challenges. Life is full of unexpected events and stressors. Resilience equips you with the mental and emotional tools to handle stress more effectively. Instead of being overwhelmed, resilient individuals can maintain their composure, think clearly, and find solutions.

Resilience isn't just about survival; it's about thriving. It allows you to see challenges as opportunities for growth and development. This mindset fosters continuous improvement and helps you learn from experiences, making you stronger and more adaptable. Building resilience contributes to better mental health. It reduces the risk of depression, anxiety, and other stress-related conditions. By developing coping mechanisms and a positive outlook, you can maintain your well-being even during tough times.

Resilient people are more likely to achieve long-term success. They persist in the face of setbacks, adapt to changing circumstances, and continue to pursue their goals. This tenacity and adaptability are key ingredients for personal and professional success.

Building resilience is closely linked to building your self-awareness. Do you go within and ask yourself questions about yourself? Becoming introspective about understanding your emotions, strengths, and areas for growth is crucial. Self-awareness is the first step in recognizing your emotional responses and managing them effectively. This involves regular self-reflection and being honest with yourself about your feelings and reactions. Journaling can be a helpful tool for this, providing a space to explore and understand your inner world.

Self-awareness is the conscious knowledge of your own character, feelings, motives, and desires. It helps you understand and manage your emotions. By recognizing what triggers certain feelings, you can develop strategies to regulate your emotions, reducing impulsive reactions and fostering emotional stability.

With self-awareness, you can make more informed decisions. Understanding your values, strengths, and weaknesses allows you to align your choices with your true self, leading to more fulfilling outcomes. Self-awareness enables you to communicate more authentically and effectively. When you know yourself, you can express your needs, boundaries, and feelings clearly. This honesty builds trust and deepens connections with others. By continually reflecting on your actions and experiences, self-awareness promotes personal growth. It encourages you to learn from your mistakes, celebrate your successes, and strive to be the best version of yourself.

Are you generally a hopeful person? Maintaining a hopeful outlook and focusing on opportunities rather than obstacles helps you resolve conflicts not just with others but within yourself. Optimism doesn't mean ignoring difficulties; it means acknowledging them while believing in your capacity to overcome them. Practice reframing negative thoughts and focusing on positive aspects to build a resilient mindset.

Do you show up for others? Cultivating strong, positive relationships that provide support, advice, and encouragement is essential. These networks offer a safety net during tough times and create a reciprocating relationship where support is mutual. Building and maintaining these connections involves being there for others, actively listening, and offering help when needed.

Problem-solving skills are not innate; we have to intentionally develop them. Most come from lessons learned from solving past issues. Developing the ability to tackle challenges head-on, find solutions, and adapt strategies as needed is a key component of resilience. This involves critical thinking, creativity, and a willingness to learn from mistakes. Engage in activities that challenge your problem-solving skills, such as puzzles, games, or even professional projects.

Building emotional resilience is a daily practice, a commitment to nurturing your well-being and growth:

1. Mindfulness and Self-Care: Regularly engaging in activities that promote mental, emotional, and physical well-being is crucial. This could include meditation, exercise, hobbies, or spending time in nature. Mindfulness helps you stay present and reduces stress, while self-care ensures you're taking time to recharge and rejuvenate.

2. Embracing Challenges as Opportunities: It is vital to view difficult situations as chances to learn, grow, and strengthen your resilience. Instead of seeing challenges as setbacks, reframe them as opportunities to develop new skills and insights. This shift in perspective can make a significant difference in how you approach and overcome obstacles.

3. Reflective Practice: Taking time to reflect on experiences, extract lessons, and apply them to future challenges is essential. Reflective practice involves regularly reviewing your actions and outcomes to understand what worked well

and what could be improved. This continuous learning process builds resilience over time.

Building Resilience and Self-Awareness

Practical Steps For Building Resilience

1. Develop a Positive Mindset

Practice optimism and focus on solutions rather than problems. Reframe negative thoughts and look for the silver lining in difficult situations. It isn't toxic positivity; it is recognizing that it could be worse and that you will overcome the current situation. Take time each day to reflect on your thoughts, feelings, and actions. Journaling can be a helpful tool for this.

2. Strengthen Your Support Network

Cultivate strong relationships with friends, family, and colleagues. Seek out those who support and encourage you, and be there for them in return. Building a support system is healthy, not needy. People need people. Identify your people.

3. Practice Stress-Management Techniques

Engage in activities that reduce stress, such as exercise, meditation, or hobbies. Find what works for you and make it a regular part of your routine. Hobbies or interests are not corny time wasters. They help produce healthy hormones in the body that help fight disease and promote a longer life span.

4. **Learn from Experience**

Reflect on past challenges and how you overcame them. Identify the strategies that worked and apply them to future situations. Don't beat yourself if a strategy half worked or didn't work. Replay it and do the introspective work to grow from it.

5. **Set Personal Goals**

Identify your strengths and areas for improvement, and set specific, achievable goals for personal growth. Review and adjust these goals regularly as needed.

Focusing on building resilience and self-awareness can transform the way you interact with the world. These qualities not only enhance your personal well-being but also strengthen your relationships and contribute to your success in all areas of life. Embrace the journey of growth and let resilience and self-awareness be your guides.

Resilient individuals tend to acknowledge their emotions. They allow themselves to feel and express their emotions without being overwhelmed by them. They seek support and aren't afraid to reach out for help from multiple sources. Taking action to address the situation by focusing on what you can control is crucial. Often, we struggle to identify this because we believe we have more control over things than we actually do. We cannot control other people, places, or things. To proactively take control, we must identify this in real time as things are occurring. This is why pausing and intentionally listening to what belongs to us versus someone else is so important.

Emotional resilience (and recognizing what you can control) doesn't just benefit you on a personal level; it extends to your relationships, work, and overall impact on the world. It fosters a sense of inner peace, improves interactions with others, and contributes to a more compassionate, understanding society.

Takeaways

- Emotional resilience is the bedrock of navigating life's challenges with grace and strength.

- Key components of resilience include self-awareness, optimism, strong support networks, and effective problem-solving skills.

- Building resilience is an ongoing practice that involves mindfulness, embracing challenges, and reflective learning.

- The benefits of resilience extend beyond personal well-being, enhancing relationships, and contributing to a positive societal impact.

Enriched Reader Prompts

1. Reflect on a Past Challenge: Think about a difficult situation you've faced. What strengths helped you through it? What did you learn about your resilience? Reflecting on past experiences can help you recognize your resilience and understand how to apply it to future challenges.

2. Daily Resilience Journal: For one week, note down any challenges you encounter and how you respond to them. Reflect on what strategies were effective and what you might do differently next time. This practice can help you identify patterns and improve your resilience over time.

3. Gratitude Practice: Each day, identify and write down three things you're grateful for. Notice how this practice influences your outlook and resilience over time. Gratitude shifts your focus to positive aspects of life, building a resilient and optimistic mindset.

Chapter 7

Implementing Boundaries

In recent years, self-care and boundaries have become synonymous. While they share a collective space in our wellness toolkit, let's talk about why boundaries matter, how to set them, and how to enforce them effectively. Life is a delicate dance between nurturing ourselves and fostering connections with others. Knowing when to draw the line and when to extend a hand can be a toss-up if you are not self-aware. This chapter explores the art of setting healthy boundaries—a practice that not only honors our own needs and values but also respects and enriches our relationships.

Boundaries are the invisible lines we draw around our emotional, physical, and mental selves. From this day forward, consider boundaries as your personal tool—a tool to help you define what is acceptable and what isn't, guiding you on how to teach people to treat you. Boundaries are meant to be healthy; however, others may label them as barriers, and some might believe they are used to manipulate. They are to be used to cultivate relationships that foster mutual respect, empathy, understanding, and support. Below are the types of boundaries we will discuss.

- **Emotional Boundaries:** Protecting your emotional space is essential for maintaining mental well-being and healthy relationships. By setting clear emotional boundaries, you create a safe zone where you can express your feelings without fear of being overwhelmed or dismissed. This involves being able to communicate your emotional needs effectively to others, ensuring that your emotional health remains a priority while also respecting the emotional boundaries of those around you.

- **Physical Boundaries:** Safeguarding your personal space, how you're touched, and your physical privacy is vital for nurturing respect and trust in relationships. Whether it's about personal space in professional settings or physical intimacy in close relationships, establishing these boundaries helps ensure that you feel safe, comfortable, and in control of your body and environment. Clear physical boundaries also signal to others what behaviors are acceptable and what aren't, helping to prevent misunderstandings and promote mutual respect. This is how you teach others how to treat you.

- **Mental Boundaries:** Guarding your thoughts and beliefs helps preserve your sense of self and intellectual integrity. You should be able to engage in respectful discussions and debates without feeling pressured to conform or change your core beliefs. Mental boundaries help you maintain control over your own thoughts and opinions, ensuring that conversations remain respectful and constructive rather than becoming overwhelming or invasive.

Boundaries are your protective shields. They help prevent burnout, stress, and resentment by ensuring you are not overextended or taken advantage of. Boundaries foster respect and understanding in relationships. They help establish clear expectations and prevent misunderstandings and conflicts. Setting and maintaining boundaries reinforces your self-worth and confidence. It sends a message that you value yourself and expect others to do the same.

The first step in setting boundaries is understanding your own needs. Remember, we discussed self-awareness earlier; this is where it is put to use. Whatever values and limits you've built around your life will help you identify where to set your boundaries.

When you reflect on your values and limits, identify areas in your life where you feel overextended, disrespected, or uncomfortable. Ask yourself:

- What makes me feel drained or stressed?

- When do I feel violated or taken for granted?

- What behaviors or situations make me uncomfortable?

Once you've identified your needs, be clear about your boundaries. The "why" can remain personal to you, but when you have to enforce them, you have to be clear about where they belong. For example, if abrasive language from a partner makes you uncomfortable, communicate this assertively. Use clear, respectful statements like, "I do not like it when you talk to me like that because I feel disrespected."

Knowing where we need the boundaries and communicating them is often something different. I can recall the moment I first recognized the need for boundaries. I was in my 30's and my responsibilities were mounting. Family and friends often pulled on me without a thought of what I may have needed. Many failed to ask. I felt a lot of resentment because I knew something was missing, but I couldn't identify what it was called. It was boundaries. I lacked the ability to draw a line for myself and others. My ignorance around boundaries was hurting me. I thankfully learned to set boundaries and communicate them verbally and nonverbally.

Effective communication is key to setting boundaries. Use "I" statements to express your needs without blaming or criticizing the other person. This approach fosters understanding and respect. For example:

- "I need some quiet time in the evenings to relax and recharge."

- "I prefer not to discuss work matters during family meals."

- "Please do not ask me questions as soon as I arrive at the office. Please let me get settled first, and then I will come to ask for updates."

Consistently uphold your boundaries. If someone crosses a boundary, address it immediately. If you don't, it is assumed that you are ok with their behavior, and they will do it again. Use assertive communication to remind them of your boundaries and the consequences of not respecting them. Consistency is crucial in reinforcing your boundaries. If you are not consistent, the boundaries will be weak and likely viewed as manipulative, depending on the situation.

You must be clear about what you need. Let's imagine you are in a relationship, and your partner tends to use language that is hurtful and abrasive. At that moment, you must decide if this will be something you will tolerate. Your partner will then learn how they can and cannot speak to you based on your response or the lack thereof. This is where assertiveness works best: speaking clearly and using statements that are not offensive toward the other person. An example statement would be, "I do not like it when you use profanity when you're talking with me because I feel disrespected." In this scenario, you stated what you did not like and why, and you made your request. The assertiveness communicates confidence in your boundary and the words used were communicated respectfully. From that moment forward, you must consistently uphold that boundary. Boundaries help you create a safe and nurturing environment where all individuals feel valued and heard.

Understand that setting and maintaining boundaries isn't always smooth sailing. You may encounter resistance, guilt, or fear of conflict. Remember, setting boundaries is a form of self-respect and an act of self-care—it's not selfish but it is necessary for healthy relationships. When we start relationships with others, we have to understand that what they see as a boundary might be vastly different than what you view as a boundary. They may have never had a relationship with someone that utilizes boundaries. This may also be why your boundaries are challenged. To some, boundaries can feel controlling. You will have to decide how and when you relax a boundary. It's critical to your mental, emotional, and physical well-being. Does that person respect your boundaries? Do they believe they are necessary? Do they appreciate you reinforcing your boundaries? These are things you will have to discern how you manage your boundaries but understand that how and when they get altered is a decision you make. This should not be anyone else's decision.

Let's consider the different relationships and the boundaries that are needed. Boundaries in personal relationships ensure that both parties feel respected and valued. They help prevent codependency, where one person relies too heavily on the other for their emotional needs. Examples include:

- Setting limits on how much time you spend with certain people.

- Communicating your need for personal space and alone time.

- Expressing your feelings and needs openly and honestly.

In the workplace, boundaries help maintain professionalism and prevent burnout. They ensure that work responsibilities do not encroach on your personal life. Examples include:

- Setting clear work hours and not answering work-related calls or emails outside of these hours.

- Delegating tasks and saying no to additional responsibilities when you're already overwhelmed.

- Maintaining a professional demeanor and not sharing too much personal information with colleagues.

Boundaries in social relationships prevent you from feeling overwhelmed or drained by social obligations. Examples include:

- Limiting your attendance at social events that you don't enjoy or that leave you feeling exhausted.

- Politely declining invitations when you need time to rest or focus on other priorities.

- Setting limits on how much you share on social media and with whom.

Boundaries teach others how to treat you and what they can expect from you. They communicate your values and expectations, fostering mutual respect and understanding. Upholding boundaries increases your self-worth. It shows that you value yourself and are willing to protect your well-being. Boundaries create healthier, more balanced relationships. They ensure that both parties' needs are met and prevent resentment and conflict.

Takeaways

- Healthy boundaries are essential for self-care and nurturing relationships.

- Understanding and communicating your boundaries clearly is key to maintaining them.

- Healthy boundaries foster respect, enhance well-being, and strengthen connections.

- Navigating the challenges of setting boundaries is part of the journey toward healthier relationships and personal growth.

Enriched Reader Prompts

1. Identify one area of your life where your boundaries could be stronger. Reflect on how this affects your well-being and relationships.

2. At the end of each week, reflect on moments where you successfully maintained your boundaries and moments where you struggled. What can you learn from these experiences?

CHAPTER 8

WHAT'S WRONG WITH ANGER

Anger is often misunderstood and stigmatized. It is a fundamental human emotion, yet so many people are unwilling to express it when it rises. Whether acute or chronic, it is an emotional, physiological, and physical display of displeasure or disapproval of someone or something. It's a signal, a fierce alarm that something is amiss—be it a violation of our values and boundaries, an unmet need, or a foiled goal. This chapter aims to demystify anger, exploring its roots, its impact, and how we can harness its energy constructively.

In its simplest definition, anger is an emotion. We know it when we see it. We recognize it in others and often compare it to our own exposure or experience of anger. It is one of the most difficult emotions for people to manage. As a therapist who assists clients in identifying it, understanding it, and managing it, I have found that most people primarily use their anger to either make something happen or stop something from happening. I, like so many others, had difficulty managing my anger. When something happens, the brain goes through an immediate response to resolve (often based on irrational thought) the root of the offense expeditiously. What you are about to learn is that you do not have to neutralize every threat. I hope this allows you to exhale because I know how exhausting it is to maintain hypervigilance.

Another thing we experience due to the stigma around anger is subconsciously suppressing it. We shove it down and tell ourselves, "It will go away." Ask yourself if that has worked. Did it really go away, or did you tell yourself a narrative trying to change your mood? When you suppress your anger, you rob yourself of an opportunity to grow in self-awareness and accountability. The moment you feel discomfort, it's a sign that there's an area in your life that still needs attention or growth. When you suppress it, you are not only taking away an opportunity to express it, but you compound a pattern of passiveness and not advocating for yourself.

I want you to understand that you were conditioned to respond in ways that did not allow you to draw a healthy perspective about anger. Anger is an adaptive reaction to perceived threats. It can be intense, but it is an intensity that can and must be controlled. We have seen others act out so negatively that we create shame and guilt around being angry. Especially women who have been labeled aggressive or combative when they attempt to express their emotions. I want you to know that you can change your perspective and use anger to motivate you to change without harming yourself or others. Being angry means we are ready to fight and defend ourselves when threatened. That fight can also look like advocacy, motivation to change and to promote compromise.

There is a certain amount of anger that is necessary for survival. Anger can range from a mild annoyance to a ferocious rage. Your level of anger should match the level of threat you feel. Has that always been the case for you, or are you one of the people that stuff it down? In the past, some people have described anger as a loss of control, a demonstration of rage, and irrational behavior. Because betrayal, untruths, and accusations are part of relationships, your increased emotional intelligence, mixed with assertive communication, is required to manage your negative experiences. Just because the hurt feels intense doesn't mean you have to react with the same intensity or even exceed it. You only need to acknowledge that something doesn't sit well with you and address it accordingly. Taking a step back from the situation will allow your thoughts or perspective to recalibrate. Anger only becomes disastrous when it is not controlled or managed. Anger, used correctly, can be considered a natural resource.

Your belief about anger is deeply connected to your family of origin. Anger and aggression can play out internally or externally. When anger is projected externally, everyone around you will experience your emotional state. Remember the story I mentioned earlier about the male attacking the female? In that situation, did you feel the emotions and tension of both the abuser and the victim? Anger expressed inward may include negative inner dialogue, depriving oneself of joy and self-sabotage. Isolation and self-harm are other ways someone can express inward anger.

How do you know when you're angry? What do you do or say once you identify anger as the emotion you want to express? As a child or adolescent, how did you see adults resolve conflict? The ways in which you deal with interpersonal conflict today are a direct reflection of who and what you saw in your formative years. The examples set by the people around you are what you display today, and you've added your own spin to it. Responses can be physical, emotional, or cognitive. Some physical responses or signs of anger include pacing, clenching of the jaw, increased heartbeat, sweaty palms, breathlessness, physical trembling, and clenched fist. Emotional responses can include irritation, guilt, rage, frustration, depression, sadness, stress, resentment, and anxiety. A cognitive response to anger includes not being able to think straight, lack of concentration, and forgetfulness.

If your anger has become chronic, there is likely a level of hostility within you that may cause you to feel sad most times. It would be best if you identified what you are sad about. This can lead to excessive stress on the body, possible self-harm, physical health problems, depression, and anxiety. Poorly managed chronic mental health issues can lead to or exacerbate the following:

- Depression

- Anxiety

- Headaches

- Insomnia

- Appetite changes

- Mental confusion

- Addictive behavior

- Social isolation

It is imperative that you diligently work on effectively communicating your needs and wants and learn how to regulate yourself before you cause more damage to yourself and others. Sometimes, people experience the above because they fear the changes in relationships that will take place if they speak up. You owe it to yourself to advocate and get support to deal with the outcomes. Choosing to advocate for yourself is an act of self-love. It can and will release you of the chronic issues mentioned.

Healthy Anger Versus Unhealthy Anger

Most people have the perception that anger is always unhealthy. Anger can be healthy and unhealthy. Society has always placed a stigma around feeling and expressing anger; that thought suggests anger is equivalent to a loss of control. Because of this a couple of things happen. Some will use contrasting adjectives to express their feelings because there has been shame associated with saying, "I'm angry." I can vividly remember being chastised for using particular words as a child to express my anger toward someone. It was quite confusing because I was failing, searching for multiple ways to say it. Children often have a limited vocabulary and require guidance and education to build their vocabulary. If you, as a parent, have particular words that you do not want your children to use, you must give them alternative words that mean the same thing without the negative connotation.

As a therapist, one of the ways I encourage clients to identify this is to be keenly aware of the things that stir up negative feelings. With the recent highlights in the media about mental health (especially during the pandemic), triggers have become a household term. As stated previously, triggers are essentially reminders of negative feelings, thoughts, and experiences from a stimulus. Triggers are widely discussed with post-traumatic stress disorder (PTSD), and you might hear some people describe their experience as such when they have a strong response to something or someone.

For example, during the pandemic, I was in a car accident. The weather conditions were not the best and it happened at a busy intersection. Since then, I have experienced physiological symptoms and anxiety at the first snow of the season. Every time I have to cross that intersection, I visualize that moment when I was hit. That is an example of a trigger. Unfortunately, triggers are not typically considered positive. Typically, when we use the word nostalgia, it refers to a longing for or a recollection of pleasant memories from the past. When you interact with people and you feel a stimulus or trigger, your brain says to respond, but you must control the level and intensity of the response. Feeling it does not make it real, and just because it feels like a level 10 threat does not mean you have to meet the perceived threat with a level 10+ response. That justification and response would be unhealthy anger, leading to harmful and destructive behavior.

A healthy or constructive anger feels more like the emotion and response that fits the situation. It is proportional to the unpleasurable event. It incites change, not vengeful behavior, and it is used as a tool. It is a type of anger that is used to solve problems. For example, when someone says or does something that bothers you, you can express your feelings by telling them, "I want to address the issues right now, but when you yell, it does not feel collaborative," or "Can you please be mindful? It can make me angry when someone is dismissive to me." Healthy anger is productive, motivating, and expressed assertively (rather than aggressively). When you know how to express your feelings clearly and calmly, you save yourself (and others) a lot of stress and confusion. Expressing your anger in a constructive manner means you recognize you are angry; you know what you need or want and can verbalize it respectfully. It is not a guarantee that you will get what you ask for, but you will be able to say you had a conversation rather than a yelling match or verbal altercation.

On the other hand, unhealthy anger is where there are high emotions and very little thought. It is destructive. When you allow the unhealthy anger to go unmanaged, your anger controls you as well as the other person. You, in turn, inflict pain on the person or people that triggered you. The truth is they do not know your triggers; they are not aware of your thoughts and feelings, and sometimes they, too, have some difficult emotions to manage. Even if the other person is aware of your triggers because you've expressed them in the past, they are not responsible for managing them; you are. Unhealthy anger is selfish, aggressive, suppressive, and passive-aggressive.

Anger manifests in various forms, from mild irritation to intense fury. Understanding these nuances is key to managing our responses:

1. Irritation: The low hum of frustration over minor annoyances.

2. Frustration: A festering sense of injustice or unfairness, often linked to past experiences.

3. Enraged: This is likely the stage where threats are made, and a person is confrontational.

4. Rage: The eruption of anger, overwhelming and often disproportionate to the trigger.

Unchecked anger can have profound effects on our well-being, relationships, and decision-making. It doesn't occur in a vacuum. Because things like personal violations, unmet expectations, and feelings of powerlessness can rise, it makes sense that there's so much intensity involved. It can erode trust, hinder communication, and lead to regrettable actions. When our personal boundaries or values are breached, there is a ripple effect, but there's also room for change.

Anger, when acknowledged and directed purposefully, can be a catalyst for positive change. It can:

1. Motivate Action: Propel us to address injustices or pursue goals.

2. Enhance Communication: When expressed assertively, it can clarify our needs and expectations.

3. Foster Self-Understanding: Serve as a mirror reflecting our deeper values and concerns.

Strategies for Managing Anger

1. Pause and Reflect: Give yourself a moment to cool down and assess the situation objectively.

2. Express Assertively: Communicate your feelings clearly and respectfully, without aggression.

3. Seek Solutions: Focus on resolving the underlying issue rather than dwelling on the anger.

Developing the ability to navigate our anger with flexibility and awareness—emotional agility—allows us to respond to life's challenges with wisdom and compassion.

Takeaways

- Anger is a complex emotion with various forms and triggers, serving as a signal of underlying issues.

- Understanding the impact of unmanaged anger is crucial for personal and relational well-being.

- Constructive channeling of anger can lead to positive outcomes, including motivation, clear communication, and self-understanding.

- Emotional agility in managing anger involves pausing, expressing ourselves assertively, and seeking solutions.

Enriched Reader Prompts

1. Anger Reflection: Recall a recent incident when you felt angry. Identify the trigger and the underlying need or value that was threatened.

2. Assertive Expression Practice: Write down a script for how you could express your anger assertively in a similar situation in the future.

3. Solution-Oriented Approach: Think of a current situation that's causing you anger. Brainstorm potential solutions that address the root cause rather than the emotion itself.

CHAPTER 9

BUILDING UP THE PARTS OF YOU

We've all been there, haven't we? Armed with new knowledge about ourselves and then stuck. There's often a gap between understanding how you've grown and walking in the growth. This chapter is about strategies on how to build a new you—from insight to action, from awareness to transformation.

The path to change is seldom straight. It's covered with obstacles—old habits, fear of the unknown, and the comfort of the familiar. Perceiving these obstacles not as roadblocks but as part of the journey will help to overcome them. Your journey will require you to embrace two things:

1. Mindset Shifts: Where you cultivate a growth mindset and view challenges as opportunities to learn and grow.

2. Emotional Resilience: Where you lean into your emotional resilience and embrace setbacks as building blocks.

What you do not control controls you. If steps are not taken to manage your thoughts and emotions, you will continue to experience and express emotional dysregulation with those around you and within yourself. Awareness creates choice. What you are looking for is a transformation that leads to you being able to harness your emotions and not "wear them on your sleeve." You want to express yourself in healthier ways, and you want your words to have an impact that yields optimal outcomes. You want to be heard. Seeing as though you've gotten this far, that tells me you have decided to take steps to manage yourself better. The rest of this chapter is the beginning of your "how."

We have thinking patterns that drive most of our behavior. The patterns are learned along the way, even after our family of origin has groomed us. Rarely do we fully dissect these patterns or discuss how they came to be—whether they serve us well or perpetuate harm, we just go into the world and spread what we think to be true. Below, we will review a list of common thinking errors that we bring to our interactions with others. These thinking errors can trap you in a toxic cycle that will take your personal and professional growth on a detour.

All-or-Nothing Thinking: Have you ever found yourself in a stage of a relationship where you felt it was either heading toward commitment or you just didn't want to be involved at all? This 'all-or-nothing' mindset can set us up for disappointment, as it would require someone to give you a guarantee of a linear experience, and relationships often have ups and downs. Embracing the gray areas and acknowledging that peaks and valleys are part of the journey can help us build stronger, more resilient bonds with our partners.

Overgeneralization: Having one negative experience with a colleague, friend, or family member doesn't mean that all future interactions with others will be the same. Overgeneralizing from one situation to another can prevent you from seeing the uniqueness in each person or relationship. Every interaction comes with its own set of challenges, but how you approach and handle those challenges is what helps relationships grow and evolve.

Mental Filter: If you find yourself focusing solely on a single mistake someone made while ignoring all the good they've done, you're falling into a mental filter. It's like viewing the relationship through a lens that only emphasizes the negatives. To maintain a healthy perspective, balance your view by recognizing the positive contributions others make in your life, whether they are friends, colleagues, or family members.

Disqualifying the Positive: If you brush off compliments, praise, or good deeds from others because of a past conflict or a challenging situation, you're disqualifying the positive. This tendency can make relationships seem more strained than they actually are. Even during difficult times, it's important to appreciate the positive qualities of the people you interact with to foster healthier, more constructive relationships.

Jumping to Conclusions: Assuming that a friend, coworker, or family member is upset with you without directly asking them creates unnecessary tension. This is a classic case of jumping to conclusions. Rather than assuming the worst, open up a line of communication to clarify misunderstandings and ensure everyone is on the same page.

Magnification or Minimization: Blowing a situation out of proportion or minimizing someone's feelings, whether in a work, social, or family context, can distort the reality of your relationship. Whether you're exaggerating a small issue or downplaying someone's achievements or concerns, finding a balanced perspective will help foster healthier, more grounded relationships.

Emotional Reasoning: Feeling rejected or overlooked in a relationship—whether it's with a friend, coworker, or family member—doesn't necessarily mean you are being rejected. Emotional reasoning can lead you to interpret feelings as facts. It's important to communicate openly and check in with the reality of the situation, ensuring that your emotions aren't clouding your judgment of the relationship.

Should Statements: Believing that others 'should' know what you need or expect without expressing it can lead to unnecessary frustration and resentment. Whether in a professional, social, or family relationship, these 'should' statements create unrealistic expectations. Clear communication about your needs and desires is far more effective in building understanding and reducing conflict.

Labeling and Mislabeling: Calling someone 'incompetent' or 'selfish' after a disagreement or misunderstanding is an example of labeling. This reduces people to a single action and overlooks the complexity of their behaviors and intentions. Focus on specific actions and how they affect you rather than assigning generalized labels that can harm relationships.

Personalization: If you often feel responsible for someone else's bad mood or difficult day, you might be personalizing their emotions. Whether it's a colleague, friend, or family member, it's important to remember that you're not responsible for everything they feel. Encourage open dialogue to understand the root cause of their emotions without taking unnecessary blame.

Now what, right? Insight is like a spark that lights up our brain, shedding light on our patterns, triggers, and the whys of our behaviors. But what do we do with that light? How do we ensure it leads us forward, not just inward? Understanding errors like these is the first step toward transforming your ability to engage in meaningful conversations and manage your emotions.

So, let's see where learning those thinking errors can take us. I want you to review the diagram below. This is a depiction of the pieces that encapsulate your life. If you had to lay out the parts of you that create a whole life, these parts are a pretty good representation. When you are rebuilding and restructuring your life, it's a good idea to consider the parts. Where are you? Where do you want to be? What support is needed for you to move these parts into position to help you change your mindset and thrive?

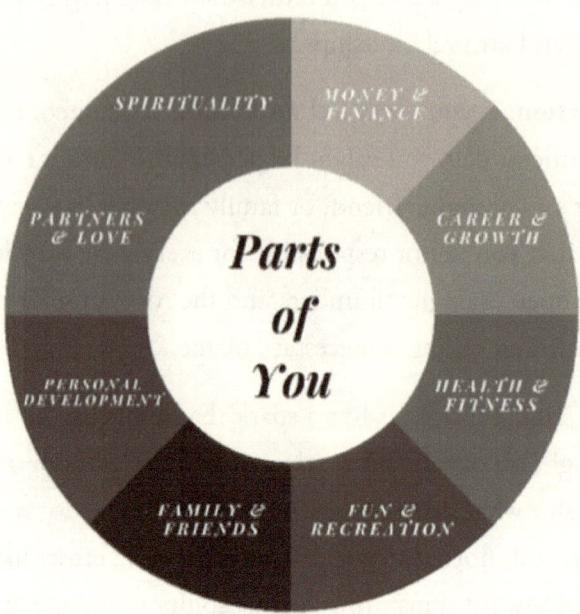

It would be great to live a life where there is growth in all of these parts. At my most tumultuous time in life, all of these parts were under attack. I experienced despair because nothing was where it was supposed to be. When I sat down and listed these pieces and realized I had to create motion, I asked those very questions above. So, let's break down these parts.

Money and Finance is always a stressor. Look at your relationship with money and how you may have learned some unhealthy habits. Your money has a job to do for you. Is it functioning the way you need it to? If not, who can help you create a financial plan? Ask those you trust to help you plan your roadmap to financially healthy habits.

Career and Growth are touchy sometimes. If you have struggled with knowing what you want to do with your professional life, you likely have a level of dreams deferred, shame, or insecurity. It does not matter where you are today. Make a plan to start fulfilling this sector of your life. This will not change without you changing it.

Health and Fitness are scary because there are quite a few things we can't control here. I want you to focus on what you CAN control. While talking with a friend one day about our weight, I gave her plenty of excuses. She then said, "Haven't we had enough cupcakes and ice cream, though?" I could not argue with that. Afterward, there was an internal dialogue that made me do different. You are in control of what you eat. You cannot "treat" yourself for everything. You are not a puppy in need of positive reinforcement. Stop rewarding yourself with food. Stop drowning your stress and sadness in food. That's not the fix you need. The fix will come from you making a decision.

Fun and Recreation are just that—stop and smell the roses. If you are sitting in the house because no one asked you to come out, you have no significant other, or you feel abandoned by whomever, this is your reminder to get up and immerse your five senses into life. Don't punish yourself by isolating. This is where you can reward yourself after working hard, caregiving, paying the bills, and driving the distance. Go get outside and remove all that is needed for you to recharge.

Family and Friends are supposed to be your support system. If you need to move some people around for the sake of your being able to thrive...do it. Don't be afraid to reclassify some people. Put some boundaries in place and create the team you need.

Personal Development is just that, personal. Going quiet and working on a goal in private is perfectly healthy. There's a time and place to share or ask for assistance. Read, research, and redefine as often as you need to. Take the class(es), go to the conference, network to raise your net worth, join the group, and get what you need to thrive.

Partners and Love tend to weigh people down because you likely want something you don't currently have. This is your reminder to assess your relationship(s) as often. Check in with the other person to ensure each of you is satisfied. Communicate your needs, thoughts, and desires, and respectfully ask for more of what you need. Listen closely to whether they will be able to meet you halfway. Are they your cheerleader or your dead weight? Only you know. Only you know the changes you need to make. Don't allow fear of change to be the reason you stay in a relationship that is no longer serving you. You get to decide.

And lastly, **spirituality,** while a very personal thing, always requires exploration. You have to ask yourself what you use to govern your life. What gives you foundation and grounding? What centers your world and brings you to a place of peace when things become chaotic? Wherever you are in your spiritual journey, know that it is a personal journey and can only be developed by you.

The journey of change begins when you commit to turning your newfound understanding into tangible steps forward.

Let's delve into a practical method that can help you decide which thoughts and behaviors to keep, which to tweak, and which to trash. I call this the "Trash It, Keep It, or Tweak It" method.

The "Trash It, Keep It, or Tweak It" Method

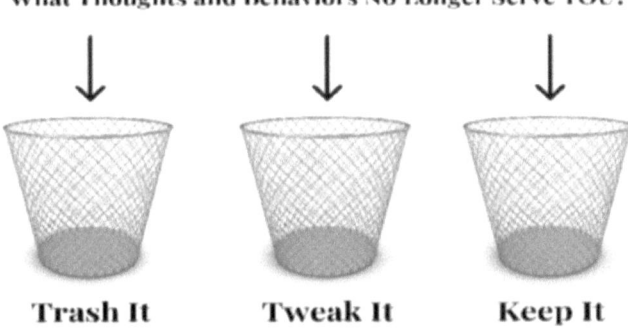

This method is a straightforward yet powerful tool for evaluating your thoughts and behaviors. By categorizing them into these three groups—trash, keep, or tweak—you can take control of your life, guiding you to healthier communication and better emotional regulation.

Step 1: Identifying Your Thoughts and Behaviors

Before you can decide what to trash, keep, or tweak, you need to identify the thoughts and behaviors that influence your communication and emotional responses. This involves self-reflection and honesty. Here are some prompts to get you started:

- How are you likely to respond to negative stimuli?

- Why do you feel the need to defend or correct people's opinions?

- Are there recurring patterns in your interactions that lead to conflict or misunderstanding?

I encourage you to write down your thoughts and behaviors as they occur so you do not blend situations. This will give you a clear picture of what you're working with.

Step 2: Evaluating Your Thoughts and Behaviors

Once you have a list, it's time to evaluate each item. Ask yourself the following questions:

- Is this thought or behavior helping or hurting my communication and emotional regulation?

- Does it align with my values and goals?

- Is it based on reality or distorted by a thinking error?

Step 3: Categorizing Your Thoughts and Behaviors

Now, let's categorize each thought and behavior in all the areas of your life you saw on the wheel:

Trash It

These are the thoughts and behaviors that are unproductive, harmful, or based on significant thinking errors. If they seem to be your go-to responses and others have complained of the same thing, they don't serve your well-being or your relationships. For example:

- Negative self-talk: "I'm not good enough."

- Catastrophizing: "This conversation will ruin everything."

- Blaming: "It's all their fault."

Trashing these thoughts and behaviors involves acknowledging their presence and consciously deciding to let them go. This might require practicing mindfulness, seeking therapy, or using affirmations to replace negative thoughts with positive ones. They likely came from a place of acute or chronic unresolved emotional pain.

Keep It

These are the thoughts and behaviors that are healthy, constructive, and align with your values and goals. During interactions, you walk away with a sense of empowerment and resolve. They contribute to effective communication and emotional regulation. For example:

- Positive self-talk: "I can handle this."

- Seeking solutions: "How can we work together to solve this issue?"

- Taking responsibility: "I can see my part in this situation."

Keeping these thoughts and behaviors means reinforcing them. Celebrate your positive patterns and continue to practice them regularly.

Tweak It

These are the thoughts and behaviors that are somewhat useful but need adjustment to become fully effective. They might be partially based on reality but distorted by minor thinking errors, or they could be healthy behaviors that need a slight change in approach. You also have to be mindful of who, when, and where. Sometimes we are responding to those around us that may not be good for us. Regulate your emotions so you can make the changes necessary to know that it may not be you in that moment. For example:

- Overgeneralizing: Instead of thinking, "I always mess up," tweak it to, "Sometimes I make mistakes, but I can learn from them."

- Emotional reasoning: Instead of, "I feel anxious, so this must be bad," tweak it to, "I feel anxious, but that doesn't necessarily mean something bad will happen."

- Assertiveness: Instead of passive-aggressively hinting at what you want, tweak it to direct and respectful communication.

Tweaking also involves refining your thoughts and behaviors to make them more balanced and effective. This might require practicing new skills, seeking feedback from others, or using cognitive-behavioral techniques to challenge and modify distorted thinking.

Step 4: Implementing Changes

Deciding what to trash, keep, or tweak is only the beginning. Implementing these changes requires consistent effort and practice. Here are some tips to help you integrate these changes into your daily life:

- *Practice mindfulness*: Stay aware of your thoughts and behaviors throughout the day. This awareness will help you catch unproductive patterns early.

- *Seek support*: Talk to a trusted friend, coach, or therapist about your progress. They can provide valuable feedback and encouragement.

- *Be patient*: Change takes time. Be patient with yourself and celebrate small victories along the way.

- *Reflect regularly*: Take time to reflect on your progress. Adjust your approach as needed and continue refining your thoughts and behaviors.

By consciously evaluating and categorizing your thoughts and behaviors, you can make meaningful changes that enhance your communication skills and emotional well-being.

Here are a few more strategies for embarking on the journey:

1. Setting Intentions: Begin with clear, purposeful intentions. What specific changes do you seek in your life? How will these changes align with your values and goals?

2. Small, Sustainable Steps: Transformative change often starts with the smallest steps. Identify actionable, manageable changes you can make in your daily routine that align with your larger intentions.

3. Accountability and Support: Share your goals with someone you trust. Accountability can significantly bolster your commitment to change.

Takeaways

- Bridging the gap between insight and action is crucial for meaningful personal change.

- Setting clear intentions and taking small, sustainable steps are vital strategies for initiating change.

- There are dimensions to your life. Review them and adjust accordingly.

- Navigating obstacles with a growth mindset and emotional resilience is essential for maintaining momentum.

- There's a system of trashing, keeping, or tweaking the parts that heal or hurt.

- Celebrating progress, no matter how small, reinforces commitment to the journey of change.

Enriched Reader Prompts

1. Intention Setting: Reflect on a key insight you've gained about yourself. What is one intention you can set that aligns with this insight? Outline the first small step you can take toward this intention.

2. Obstacle Mapping: Identify potential obstacles you might face in implementing this change. How can you navigate or mitigate these obstacles?

3. Progress Journal: Keep a weekly journal of your journey. Note the steps you've taken, the obstacles you've encountered, and how you've overcome them. Celebrate each week's progress, no matter how modest.

Chapter 10

Putting It All Together

As we come to the close of this book, remember that this is not an ending—it's the start of a transformation. Over the course of these chapters, we have explored the depths of emotions, communication, boundaries, and personal growth. You've gained insights into recognizing your communication patterns, breaking unhelpful cycles, regulating your emotions, and navigating the complexities of anger and relationships. Each chapter has provided tools not just for understanding yourself but for enhancing your interactions with others, whether in personal, social, or professional settings.

In **Chapter 1**, we uncovered the language of emotions and how they shape our communication. **Chapter 2** introduced the idea of creating your personal communication blueprint, while **Chapter 3** tackled the challenge of breaking cycles and reshaping learned behaviors. We discussed the **conversational pitfalls** many of us fall into in **Chapter 4** and explored **active listening** as a crucial life skill in **Chapter 5**. **Chapter 6** highlighted **emotional regulation** as the key to empathy and understanding, and **Chapter 7** emphasized the importance of setting and respecting boundaries. In **Chapter 8**, we unraveled anger and how it affects our lives, culminating in **Chapter 9**, where we discussed rebuilding **yourself**—the flexibility to handle life's emotional ups and downs with resilience and grace.

Now, as you embark on the **30-Day Transformation**, remember that growth is an ongoing journey. This guide is designed to help you apply the principles from the book, one step at a time. Each day presents a new opportunity to deepen your self-awareness, improve your communication, and strengthen your relationships. From journaling about your emotional triggers to practicing active listening and setting boundaries, these daily tasks are your roadmap for lasting change. **Intentionality**, **mindfulness**, and **adaptability** will be your companions throughout this process.

For some, this transformation may call for additional support. Engaging in **therapy** can be a powerful next step. Just as I have shared my own experiences and challenges in this book, therapists offer a safe space for you to explore your feelings, develop new coping mechanisms, and gain clarity. Therapy isn't about someone solving your problems—it's about having a partner in your growth journey who provides insights, tools, and encouragement along the way.

Whether you are a student, a professional, or simply someone seeking personal growth, this book can serve as a resource in various aspects of life. **In schools**, educators can use it to promote emotional intelligence and communication skills, helping students navigate their feelings and interactions. **In companies**, this book can be a tool for team building, fostering open communication, setting healthy boundaries, and creating emotionally intelligent workplaces. **In personal relationships**, it can guide you through the highs and lows of connection, helping you develop healthier, more resilient bonds.

So, whether you're using this book to better understand your emotions, build stronger professional relationships, or enhance communication with your loved ones, the transformation is yours to create. And this journey doesn't end with these 30 days—it's an invitation to continue growing, learning, and evolving.

Your path to a balanced, more fulfilling life is in your hands. Stay committed to the process, and remember: every step, no matter how small, is progress.

Thank you for trusting me to guide you through this exploration of communication in relationships. The steps you take from here will shape the richness of your interactions and the depth of your connections. Here's to your continued growth and the thriving relationships ahead!

30-DAY
TRANSFORMATION GUIDE

CHANGING BEHAVIORS FOR A BALANCED LIFE

As we conclude this journey, understand it's not an end but a beginning—a launchpad for the transformative journey that lies ahead. This 30-day challenge is your blueprint for growth, a daily commitment to applying the principles we've explored not just to envision but embody the change we seek. So, let's set the stage!

1. Intentionality: Approach each day with purpose, aligning your actions with your broader goals for growth.

2. Mindfulness: Stay present in each task, each interaction, and each moment of reflection.

3. Adaptability: Be prepared to adjust your approach as you learn what works best for you in different contexts.

Week 1

Self-Awareness and Emotional Regulation

- Day 1: Journal about your emotional triggers and the feelings they evoke.

- Day 2: Practice mindfulness meditation, focusing on your breath and bodily sensations.

- Day 3: Identify and reflect on a recent situation where you could have regulated your emotions more effectively.

- Day 4: Try a new stress-relief activity, such as yoga, walking, or swimming.

- Day 5: Write down three strengths and three areas for growth in your emotional intelligence.

- Day 6: Engage in an empathy-building activity, like volunteering or helping a friend in need.

- Day 7: Reflect on the week's insights and progress. Journal about your experiences and learnings.

Week 2

Communication Skills Enhancement

- Day 8: Practice active listening in all your conversations, focusing fully on the speaker.

- Day 9: Use "I" statements in a discussion to express your feelings and needs clearly.

- Day 10: Engage in a difficult conversation with someone, aiming for clarity and empathy.

- Day 11: Offer constructive feedback to a colleague or friend, focusing on specific behaviors and impacts.

- Day 12: Ask for feedback on your communication style from someone you trust.

- Day 13: Write a letter to express something you've found challenging to say in person.

- Day 14: Reflect on the week's communication challenges and achievements. What did you learn about your communication style?

Week 3

Building and Maintaining Healthy Relationships

- Day 15: Identify a relationship you'd like to strengthen. Reach out to the person to express appreciation.

- Day 16: Set a boundary in a relationship where you've felt overextended.

- Day 17: Plan a quality time activity with a loved one, focusing on meaningful interaction.

- Day 18: Practice forgiveness by not focusing on a minor grudge or misunderstanding.

- Day 19: Engage in a collaborative activity, focusing on teamwork and mutual respect.

- Day 20: Reflect on a relationship that challenges you. Journal about ways you can improve your interactions.

- Day 21: Review your relationship goals and the progress you've made toward them.

Week 4

Integration and Application

- Day 22: Choose one key insight from the past three weeks to apply in a new way today.

- Day 23: Create a personal mantra or affirmation that encapsulates your growth journey. Use it throughout the day. I've personally practiced, "I am going to have a peaceful day, and no one will interrupt that."

- Day 24: Teach someone else a concept or skill you've learned from this challenge.

- Day 25: Face a fear or challenge that's been holding you back, using the skills you've developed.

- Day 26: Plan a self-care day (not a list of appointments that can be mistaken for upkeep or grooming) that incorporates practices from the challenge.

- Day 27: Reflect on the changes you've noticed in yourself and your interactions with others.

- Day 28-30: For the final three days, combine elements from each week in a way that feels holistic and representative of your growth. Reflect on your journey and the changes you've experienced, and set intentions for continuing your growth beyond the challenge.

www.ingramcontent.com/pod-product-compliance
Lightning Source LLC
Chambersburg PA
CBHW021120130626
46554CB00002B/783